Abide in Him

A Theological Interpretation of John's First Letter

A. Blake White

Books By
A. Blake White

∞

Galatians: A Theological Interpretation
The Law of Christ: A Theological Proposal
The Newness of the New Covenant
Union with Christ

Abide in Him

A Theological Interpretation of John's First Letter

A. Blake White

NEW COVENANT MEDIA

5317 Wye Creek Drive, Frederick, MD 21703-6938
301-473-8781 | info@newcovenantmedia.com
www.NewCovenantMedia.com

Abide in Him:
A Theological Interpretation of John's First Letter

Published by: New Covenant Media
                5317 Wye Creek Drive
                Frederick, Maryland 21703-6938

Orders: www.newcovenantmedia.com

Printed in the United States of America

ISBN 13: 978-1-928965-40-4

To Josiah,

Dear son,

Keep yourself from idols (1 John 5:21)

Table of Contents

Foreword

John G. Reisinger

The apostle John is very explicit in stating his purpose for writing both his gospel (John 20:30, 31) and his first epistle (1 John 5:13). These two passages are clear. In the gospel of John, he is writing to unbelievers in the hope they will believe and be saved. In his first epistle, John is writing to give assurance to those who believe but are not sure their faith is sincere.

There are two very wrong approaches to 1 John. The first uses 1 John 5:13 to prove that assurance of salvation is possible and then goes to texts in the gospel of John, like John 3:16, to give assurance to everyone who professes to believe. When John says, *"**These things** have I written unto you that believe that you may know that you have eternal life,"* he is not talking about the things recorded in the gospel of John. He is talking about the things in First John. He is not talking about John 3:16 where it is promised that all who believe will receive eternal life. He is talking about the tests of true faith, such as *"Hereby we know we love God because we keep his commandments"* in 1 John 2:2-4.

There are two extremes that must be avoided when preaching 1 John. First, we must not use it merely to prove that assurance of salvation is possible and ignore the clear tests of true saving faith. This will lead to easy believism, which soon becomes antinominianism. The mentality and life style of present day fundamentalism is an example of this error. The second error is applying texts like 1 John 2:2-4 in such a way as to deny New Covenant Theology, put the conscience under law, and leave the believer with no assurance. I heard a lengthy series of sermons where each sermon was designed to destroy assurance unless the individual was near sinless perfection. I remember thinking that only a deluded die-hard legalist could twist a series of passages designed to give assurance of salvation into verses that destroyed assurance. Blake White in his commentary on 1 John has clearly avoided both of the above errors.

A good exegesis of a passage of Scripture, especially the New Testament epistles, will do the following. First, it will explain why the passage was written. Exactly what was the problem at the time of the writing that the author was dealing with? Second, how does the passage deal with and answer the problem? Third, how is the problem dealt with similar to a problem we face today? Fourth, how does the truth in the passage help us with our problem today? Again, the author has done this successfully.

Another mark of a good commentary is the author's willingness to tackle the difficult sections. Blake has a lengthy and clear exposition of the "Rock of Gibraltar" text (*"...he is the propitiation for the sins of the whole world..."* 1 John 2:2) used by Arminian universal atonement people (see pages 35-46). Another example is 1 John 3:9, *"Whosoever is born of God doth not commit sin; for his seed remaineth in him: and he cannot sin, because he is born of God."* This is the favorite text of the holiness people. The author shows the clear distinction between eternal security ("once saved, always saved" regardless of how you live) and biblical perseverance of the saints.

What are we to do with 1 John 3:6-7? This is a striking statement from John. He has already stated that the person who says he has no sin is a liar and the truth is not in him (1 John 1:8-10). John is referring to habitual sin here. This is the view of the ESV and NIV, which translates the literal "everyone who abides in him does not sin" as "no one who abides in him keeps on sinning" to signify the continual nature of sin. John is not speaking of perfection but of the pattern and direction of a person's life. Christians fall into sin; they do not dive into it or walk into it (pages 78-79).

The author's New Covenant convictions are evident throughout the book. One example is his discussion of the word *commandments*. He insists, as consistent New Covenant Theology always does, that obedience to the revealed will of God is an essential proof that we truly love God and are one of his redeemed. This fact is not debatable. Exactly where we find the will of God revealed is a matter of great difference in Reformed circles today.

John now applies the first test: obedience. Do the false teachers know the Lord? How do we know that we know the Lord? John's answer is that we know we know him if we keep his commandments.... One who claims to know the Lord but is not obeying his commandments is a liar....

It must be asked, "What commandments are John speaking of?" First, John uses the word *commandments* 14 times. The fundamental commandment is to believe in the name of Jesus Christ (1 John 3:23), but belief never stays "in the air." If it is to be biblical, it must hit the ground running. We tend to have a Greek view of faith, rather than a Hebrew view. Faith is fundamentally receptive in receiving salvation, but it never stays passive. It gets busy from the beginning. Faith *works* (Gal. 5:6, Rom. 1:5).

There is no hint in this letter, or in any of John's writings, that he is referring to the Mosaic law (page 49).

1 John has a lot to say about loving the world. The author avoids the usual temptation to make worldliness mean whatever happens to be the individual pet whipping boy at

the moment. When I was first converted, going to movies and smoking were among the most grievous sins. I remember hearing a Southern preacher on the radio speaking on "love not the world." He was doing a pretty good job until he got to defining what worldliness was. He said, "And what is God talking about in this verse? What is worldliness? Any truly spiritually minded person will know that God is talking about playing baseball." He then went into a tirade against baseball. Blake connects worldliness with a heart that does not know how to share the goods God has given us.

A good way to see if you are worldly is to look at your bank accounts and credit cards. Do you buy things you do not have the money for? We have invented a civilized and more positive term for debt, namely credit.

Greed is basically a problem of vision. The urge to be rich will never go away in this age so we must redirect the desire to be rich in this life. We should rather strive to be rich in the age to come, storing up treasures in heaven. What is the opposite of greed? Giving. Seek to become a generous person. The best way to combat greed is by giving generously (page 64).

A. W. Tozer said, "It is not what you own that is important but what owns you. You can own five cars as long as none of them own you." 1 John 3 is quite clear on the true meaning of love.

17 *But if anyone has the world's goods and sees his brother in need, yet closes his heart against him, how does God's love abide in him? 18 Little children, let us not love in word or talk but in deed and in truth.*

John does not leave us in the abstract about love. It is easy to *say* we will lay down our lives for our brothers and sisters because the reality of that happening is rare.

The switch from the plural *brothers* in verse 16 to the singular *brother* in verse 17 is deliberate. It is easy to say we love "the church," without having to give of self in specific ways for specific individuals. Loving everyone may be an excuse for loving no one. Love must be prepared to meet the needs of others whatever the cost in self-sacrifice. *Goods* in verse 17 is the same word for possessions in 1 John 2:17 (*bios*).

The background of John's thinking here may be Deuteronomy 15:7-9 which reads, *"If among you, one of your brothers should become poor, in any of your towns within your land that the Lord your God is giving you, you shall not harden your heart or shut your hand against your poor brother, but you shall open your hand to him and lend him sufficient for his need, whatever it may be. Take care lest there be an unworthy thought in your heart and you say, 'The seventh year, the year of release is near,' and your eye look grudgingly on your poor brother, and you give him nothing, and he cry to the Lord against you, and you be guilty of sin"* (page 91).

If I were to pick one section of this commentary that gives the heartbeat of both the commentary and of New Covenant Theology, it would be the following:

As should be clear by now, love for John is not an emotion but is always practical and active. Love of fellow Christians expresses itself with actions and in truth. Love and obedience go hand in hand. Jesus made this clear in the Upper Room Discourse. John 14:15 says, *"If you love me, you will keep my commandments."* In John 14:21, Jesus said that the one who has and keeps his commandments is the one who loves him. John is a faithful interpreter of the mind of Jesus (page 114-115).

Chapter 1

Introduction to 1 John

Any time we approach a book of the Bible, we should ask ourselves, "Where are we at in the story?"[1] With all of the books of the New Testament except the Gospels and Acts, this is an easy question. The audience of John's letters is in the same period of redemptive history as we are. We both live on this side of the resurrection and the pouring out of the Holy Spirit. This makes interpretation and application much easier. Before we jump into the text of 1 John, it will be helpful to zoom out and get the big picture.

First John is a pastoral letter written from Ephesus probably around 80-85 AD written by John the apostle. He gives us several reasons why he is writing. First John 5:13 says, *"I write these things to you who believe in the name of the Son of God that you may know that you have eternal life."* This is similar to the reason that John gives in his gospel: *"But these are written so that you may believe that Jesus is the Christ, the Son of God,*

---

[1] For a more technical discussion of "where we are in the story," see Richard Lints' *The Fabric of Theology: A Prolegomenon to Evangelical Theology* (Grand Rapids: Eerdmans, 1993), 293ff. where he, following Ed Clowney [*Biblical Theology and Preaching* (Phillipsburg, NJ: P&R Publishing, 1961), 87ff.], lays out the "three horizons of redemptive interpretation."

and that by believing you may have life in his name." (John 20:31).[2] Why else does he write?[3]

1 John 1:4—*And we are writing these things so that our joy may be complete.*

1 John 2:1—*My little children, I am writing these things to you so that you may not sin. But if anyone does sin, we have an advocate with the Father, Jesus Christ the righteous.*

1 John 2:12—*I am writing to you, little children, because your sins are forgiven for his name's sake.*

1 John 2:21—*I write to you, not because you do not know the truth, but because you know it, and because no lie is of the truth.*

1 John 2:26—*I write these things to you about those who are trying to deceive you.*

John writes to give assurance to the faithful believers and to expose false believers. John does not write in a linear fashion like the apostle Paul. There is no traceable argument. Instead, he takes up five themes and returns to them again and again:[4]

1. The Authority and Truthfulness of the Early Traditions

1 John 1:1—*That which was from the beginning, which we have heard, which we have seen with our eyes, which we looked upon and have touched with our hands, concerning the word of life—*

1 John 2:7—*Beloved, I am writing you no new commandment, but an old commandment that you had from the beginning. The old commandment is the word that you have heard.*

---

[2] Frank Thielman, *Theology of the New Testament* (Grand Rapids: Zondervan, 2005), 536.

[3] See John Piper, *Finally Alive* (Scotland: Christian Focus, 2009), 124-25.

[4] Thielman, *Theology of the New Testament*, 542.

1 John 2:24—*Let what you heard from the beginning abide in you. If what you heard from the beginning abides in you, then you too will abide in the Son and in the Father.*

2. The Witness of the Traditions to Jesus' Humanity

1 John 1:1-3—*That which was from the beginning, which we have heard, which we have seen with our eyes, which we looked upon and have touched with our hands, concerning the word of life—the life was made manifest, and we have seen it, and testify to it and proclaim to you the eternal life, which was with the Father and was made manifest to us—that which we have seen and heard we proclaim also to you, so that you too may have fellowship with us; and indeed our fellowship is with the Father and with his Son Jesus Christ.*

Notice the emphasis in this single Greek sentence. They heard, saw, looked at, touched, saw, saw, and heard. John wants his readers to be clear. They were eyewitnesses of the incarnate Christ.

3. The Witness of the Traditions to the Relationship between the Christian and Sin

1 John 1:8—*If we say we have no sin, we deceive ourselves, and the truth is not in us. If we confess our sins, he is faithful and just to forgive us our sins and to cleanse us from all unrighteousness. If we say we have not sinned, we make him a liar, and his word is not in us.*

4. The Witness of the Traditions to the Significance of Jesus' Death

1 John 2:2—*He is the propitiation for our sins, and not for ours only but also for the sins of the whole world.*

1 John 4:10—*In this is love, not that we have loved God but that he loved us and sent his Son to be the propitiation for our sins.*

5. The Witness of the Traditions to Love as the Proof of a Relationship with God

John is the "apostle of love." I think I have said the same thing about the apostle Paul though! This just shows how important love is in the New Testament. New Testament scholar Frank Thielman writes, "Believers demonstrate this love by remaining in fellowship with the Elder, his community, its authentic tradition, and the Father and Son to whom the tradition points."[5]

Many students of John's first letter have noted that he uses three tests throughout the letter as a double-edged sword. With these three tests, the faithful will be assured and the unfaithful exposed. They are diligently intertwined throughout. The three tests are doctrine, obedience, and love.

First, doctrine is vitally important to John (as with all the biblical authors). The doctrine that is of particular importance for John is the person of Jesus Christ. Jesus Christ came in the flesh. For example, consider the following passages:

1 John 1:1-3 — _That which was from the beginning, which we have heard, which we have seen with our eyes, which we looked upon and have touched with our hands, concerning the word of life—the life was made manifest, and we have seen it, and testify to it and proclaim to you the eternal life, which was with the Father and was made manifest to us—that which we have seen and heard we proclaim also to you, so that you too may have fellowship with us; and indeed our fellowship is with the Father and with his Son Jesus Christ._

1 John 2:22 — _Who is the liar but he who denies that Jesus is the Christ? This is the antichrist, he who denies the Father and the Son._

---

[5] Ibid., 553.

1 John 4:2—*By this you know the Spirit of God: every spirit that confesses that Jesus Christ has come in the flesh is from God…*

1 John 5:6—*This is he who came by water and blood—Jesus Christ; not by the water only but by the water and the blood. And the Spirit is the one who testifies, because the Spirit is the truth.*

1 John 5:20—*And we know that the Son of God has come and has given us understanding, so that we may know him who is true; and we are in him who is true, in his Son Jesus Christ. He is the true God and eternal life.*

The second test is obedience. Right belief must work itself out in righteousness. We see this in several passages:

1 John 1:6—*If we say we have fellowship with him while we walk in darkness, we lie and do not practice the truth.*

1 John 2:4—*Whoever says "I know him" but does not keep his commandments is a liar, and the truth is not in him.*

1 John 3:6—*No one who abides in him keeps on sinning; no one who keeps on sinning has either seen him or known him.*

1 John 3:8—*Whoever makes a practice of sinning is of the devil, for the devil has been sinning from the beginning. The reason the Son of God appeared was to destroy the works of the devil.*

1 John 3:9—*No one born of God makes a practice of sinning, for God's seed abides in him, and he cannot keep on sinning because he has been born of God.*

1 John 3:10—*By this it is evident who are the children of God, and who are the children of the devil: whoever does not practice righteousness is not of God, nor is the one who does not love his brother.*

One scholar writes, "Spurious faith does not have the right to assurance before God; genuine faith can be authenticated not only by the validity of its object (in this case, the belief that Jesus is Christ come in the flesh) but also by the transformation it effects in the individual: genuine Christians learn to love one another and obey the truth. Christian assurance is not, for John, an abstract good; it is intimately tied to a continuing and transforming relationship with the covenant God, who has revealed himself in Jesus Christ."[6]

The third test is love. Consider the following sample of passages:

1 John 2:9—*Whoever says he is in the light and hates his brother is still in darkness.*

1 John 3:10—*By this it is evident who are the children of God, and who are the children of the devil: whoever does not practice righteousness is not of God, nor is the one who does not love his brother.*

1 John 3:15—*Everyone who hates his brother is a murderer, and you know that no murderer has eternal life abiding in him.*

1 John 3:17—*But if anyone has the world's goods and sees his brother in need, yet closes his heart against him, how does God's love abide in him?*

1 John 4:20-21—*If anyone says, "I love God," and hates his brother, he is a liar; for he who does not love his brother whom he has seen cannot love God whom he has not seen. And this commandment we have from him: whoever loves God must also love his brother.*

Of course, as we will see, our love is repeatedly grounded *in being loved.*[7] In biblical theology, the imperative always *flows from* the indicative.[8] R.E.O. White writes, "Christian love is the reflex of divine love in human hearts—they who

---

[6] D.A. Carson and Douglas J. Moo, *An Introduction to the New Testament* (Grand Rapids: Zondervan, 2005), 685.

[7] Wolfgang Schrage, *The Ethics of the New Testament*, trans. David E. Green (Philadelphia: Fortress Press, 1982), 300.

[8] For more on the relationship between the indicative and the imperative, see my *The Law of Christ: A Theological Proposal* (Frederick, MD, New Covenant Media, 2010), 41-47.

have been so loved cannot help loving."[9] Wolfgang Schrage writes, "According to John, Christian duty can be summed up in a single phrase: brotherly love."[10] And of course, love is not merely an emotion, but is rather humble service of others.[11]

These three tests form the main message.[12] These three tests are diligently intertwined and stand or fall together.

John is also writing to warn (2:18, 2:26, 4:1). False teachers were in their midst. Paul had previously warned that *"I know that after my departure, fierce wolves will come in among you, not sparing the flock; and from among your own selves will arise men speaking twisted things, to draw away the disciples after them"* (Acts 20:29-30). John is writing in part because there were some opponents to the true Christian faith. John says that they are anti-Christ (1 John 2:18). Among other things, they denied that Jesus came in the flesh (1 John 4:2).

What sort of opponents were they? It is hard to say for sure, but it is safe to say that they were some sort of Platonists run wild. Platonism had lots of diversity. The church

---

[9] R.E.O. White, *Biblical Ethics* (Atlanta: John Knox Press, 1979), 199.

[10] Wolfgang Schrage, *The Ethics of the New Testament*, 314. Later he writes, "Love is clearly the highest demand, if not the sole demand, made of Christians.... Love is the sign par excellence that one belongs to the sphere of life and salvation in which the disciples dwell," 318.

[11] Richard Hays, *The Moral Vision of the New Testament* (New York: HarperOne, 1996), 144, 154; Michael J. Gorman, *Cruciformity* (Grand Rapids: Eerdmans, 2001), 160, 172, 174, 177, 178, 215, 223, 258, 379. R.E.O. White writes, "For definition of love, John's mind turns ever to obedience and to sacrifice," in *Biblical Ethics*, 197.

[12] John Stott, *The Letters of John* (Downers Grove, IL: IVP Academic, 1988), 61.

fathers traced the heresy to Simon Magus (Acts 8). The opponent that John is going after is some sort of incipient Gnosticism. Gnosticism is concerned with deliverance from the flesh by gaining knowledge. It is justification by knowledge. Docetism was a branch of Gnosticism that denied incarnation because flesh is evil. If flesh is evil, the Messiah couldn't possible have taken it on.

They also thought sinlessness was realized. They denied being subject to sin. They thought that since they believed, they were outside the sphere in which sin matters. They did not take sin seriously enough, so John mentions it frequently. This belief contributed to their neglect of the commandments. In short, they were idolaters. This explains why John closes the letter with the exhortation to his readers to guard themselves from idols (1 John 5:21). The Jesus that orthodox Christianity presents and proclaims is the true God (1 John 5:20). Any other Jesus is an idol.[13]

John combats these opponents in part by emphasizing Jesus' earthly human life. He also ties together true Christian behavior with Jesus' life. Sometimes evangelicals neglect the life of Jesus. This may be due to the fact that the ecumenical creeds tend to skip from the virgin birth to the death of Christ (born of the Virgin Mary, suffered under Pontius Pilate). His death, resurrection, and ascension are rightly emphasized, but one should never forget about the life of Jesus. John often portrays the incarnate Messiah as our example (another neglected theme of Scripture). Consider how John

---

[13] Benjamin L. Merckle, "First John 5:21 as an Interpretive Key to the Epistle," unpublished paper presented to the Evangelical Theological Society, 12.

uses the adverb *just as* (*kathōs*) in this letter and in his gospel:

1 John 2:6—*Whoever says he abides in him ought to walk **in the same way** in which he walked.*

1 John 3:3—*And everyone who thus hopes in him purifies himself **as** he is pure.*

1 John 3:7—*Little children, let no one deceive you. Whoever practices righteousness is righteous, **as** he is righteous.*

1 John 3:23—*And this is his commandment, that we believe in the name of his Son Jesus Christ and love one another, **just as** he has commanded us.*

1 John 4:17—*By this is love perfected with us, so that we may have confidence for the day of judgment, because **as** he is so also are we in this world.*

John 13:34—*A new commandment I give to you, that you love one another: **just as** I have loved you, you also are to love one another.*

John 15:10—*If you keep my commandments, you will abide in my love, **just as** I have kept my Father's commandments and abide in his love.*

John 15:12—*This is my commandment, that you love one another **as** I have loved you.*

The earthly Jesus is our example. We are to live just as he lived. One scholar writes, "God's saving act in Jesus Christ is not only a central motif, the only thing that makes Christian love possible, it is also the absolute criterion of this love.... The love displayed by Jesus is not only the basis for love within the community; it is also paradigmatic of its nature and manner.... Just as only those who are loved can love, so those who love are bound by Jesus' example of love.... Conformity to Christ and to his love determines the entire way Christians live."[14] John repeatedly stresses that Jesus is the Christ come in the flesh and that faith in him produces obedience to God's commands and love for one another.

---

[14] Schrage, *Ethics of the NT*, 306, 307, 308; cf. also White, *Biblical Ethics*, 202-03.

Chapter 2

1 John 1:1-4

That which was from the beginning, which we have heard, which we have seen with our eyes, which we looked upon and have touched with our hands, concerning the word of life—the life was made manifest, and we have seen it, and testify to it and proclaim to you the eternal life, which was with the Father and was made manifest to us—that which we have seen and heard we proclaim also to you, so that you too may have fellowship with us; and indeed our fellowship is with the Father and with his Son Jesus Christ. And we are writing these things so that our joy may be complete.

1-2 *That which was from the beginning, which we have heard, which we have seen with our eyes, which we looked upon and have touched with our hands, concerning the word of life—the life was made manifest, and we have seen it, and testify to it and proclaim to you the eternal life, which was with the Father and was made manifest to us—*

The main verb in these tangled sentences is *proclaim*. The goal of the proclamation is fellowship and joy as we will see. John uses the phrase *from the beginning* (*ap archēs*) several times in this letter, with various connections:[1]

1 John 1:1—*That which was from the beginning, which we have heard, which we have seen with our eyes, which we looked upon and have touched with our hands, concerning the word of life—*

1 John 2:7—*Beloved, I am writing you no new commandment, but an old commandment that you had from the beginning. The old commandment is the word that you have heard.*

---

[1] Colin G. Kruse, *The Letters of John* (Grand Rapids: Eerdmans, 2000), 57.

1 John 2:13—*I am writing to you, fathers, because you know him who is from the beginning. I am writing to you, young men, because you have overcome the evil one. I write to you, children, because you know the Father.*

1 John 2:14—*I write to you, fathers, because you know him who is from the beginning. I write to you, young men, because you are strong, and the word of God abides in you, and you have overcome the evil one.*

1 John 2:24—*Let what you heard from the beginning abide in you. If what you heard from the beginning abides in you, then you too will abide in the Son and in the Father.*

1 John 3:8—*Whoever makes a practice of sinning is of the devil, for the devil has been sinning from the beginning. The reason the Son of God appeared was to destroy the works of the devil.*

1 John 3:11—*For this is the message that you have heard from the beginning, that we should love one another.*

When John says "what was from the beginning," he is probably referring to the beginning of the Christian era. Some think this refers to the time before creation, as John's gospel does: *"In the beginning was the Word, and the Word was with God, and the Word was God"* (1:1). This could be a correct interpretation since we are working with the same author, but in context, this more likely refers to the beginning of the incarnation.[2]

Similarly, the word of life could refer to Jesus, the Word of John's gospel, or to the "message" of life, i.e., the gospel.[3] I tend to lean towards the former. Jesus is the word of life. He is the one they have seen and heard and touched. They did not see, hear, or touch the message of the gospel. Of course,

---

[2] Ibid., 51.

[3] Stott, *Letters of John*, 62.

one cannot separate the person of Jesus from the message about him. As Colin Kruse says, "He proclaims a message that has been embodied in a person—the person of Jesus Christ."[4]

Jesus is the Word of Life. He is the Word that gives life. As John Stott writes, "The genitive *of life* in the fourth gospel means 'life-giving' (e.g. 'light of life,' 'Bread of life' in 8:12; 6:35, 48; cf. 'living water' in John 4:10-11 and 'water of life' in Rev. 21:16; 22:1, 17)."[5]

This life was *revealed*.[6] Human beings are dependent on God's gracious self-revelation. Oh, how grateful ought we to be for the fact that God has revealed this life! John also has the false teachers in mind here. The Word was revealed. Christ became incarnate in human history. John and the apostles were eyewitnesses. They saw him, heard him, and touched him.

Eternal life probably refers to the life of the age to come (*tēn zōēn aiōnion*) as well as to Jesus, the Word of Life.[7] The reason is John says this eternal life was with the Father and

---

[4] Kruse, *Letters of John,* 53. So also I. Howard Marshall, *Epistles of John* (Grand Rapids: Eerdmans, 1978), 101. Marshall thinks John means two things which are one: both the message and Jesus.

[5] Stott, *Letters of John,* 65.

[6] As Stott puts it, "We could not have seen the one who was eternally with the Father unless he had taken the initiative deliberately to manifest himself. Human beings can apprehend only what God is pleased to make known," *Letters of John,* 65.

[7] N.T. Wright, writes, "Eternal life meant the age to come, the time when God would bring heaven and earth together, the time when God's kingdom would come and his will be done on earth as in heaven," *After You Believe* (New York: HarperOne, 2010), 13.

was revealed to us.[8] Also, in 1 John 5:20, John says Jesus *"is the true God and eternal life."*[9] First John 5:11-13 says, *"And this is the testimony, that God gave us eternal life, and this life is in his Son. Whoever has the Son has life; whoever does not have the Son of God does not have life. I write these things to you who believe in the name of the Son of God that you may know that you have eternal life."*

Eternal life is found in the Word of Life. Christians tend to think that eternal life is all future, but eternal life in John's writings often refers to life in the present as well.[10] Eternal life is certainly escaping death (1 John 3:14), but is also about the quality of life in the present. In John 10:10, Jesus said, *"I came that they may have life, and have it abundantly."* First John does not spell what eternal life is in detail, but John gives us a fuller picture. As Kruse puts it, "To have eternal life means to have one's spiritual hunger and thirst satisfied (John 4:14; 6:35); to be raised up on the last day and to live forever (John 6:40, 51, 54); to have the light of life so that one does not walk in darkness (John 8:12); to have abundant life (John 10:10); to know the only true God, and Jesus Christ whom he sent (John 17:3); and that, though we die, we will live (John 11:25)."[11]

> 3 *that which we have seen and heard we proclaim also to you, so that you too may have fellowship with us; and indeed our fellowship is with the Father and with his Son Jesus Christ.*

---

[8] Kruse, *Letters of John*, 57, 185.

[9] Cf. John 1:4, 5:26, 11:25, 14:6, 17:2.

[10] Kruse, *Letters of John*, 184.

[11] Ibid., 187.

Notice the purpose clause in this verse: They have pro-claimed the message *so that* you may have fellowship. This does not mean that his readers are not Christians. He is pre-scribing the condition for continuance in fellowship.[12]

Fellowship simply means to "have in common."[13] It is personal relationship characterized by commitment. One does not hear the word *fellowship* outside of Christian circles. Fellowship is the "common participation in the grace of God, the salvation of Christ and the indwelling Spirit which is the spiritual birthright of all believers. It is our common possession of God, Father, Son, and Holy Spirit, which makes us one." Our fellowship with each other arises from, and depends on, our fellowship with God.[14]

John calls Jesus the "Son of God" twenty-two times in this letter and unlike Paul, he does not refer to believers as sons but rather as children so as to mark the fundamental distinc-tion between the Son of God and the children of God.[15]

We see in 1 John, just like we see in every book of the Bi-ble, that right belief is vital to authentic Christianity. In other words, doctrine matters. As D.A. Carson and Douglas Moo put it, "There is no place for petty gurus in the church who will not bow to apostolic admonition and authority."[16] The apostolic testimony is authoritative. Notice the purpose clause of verse three. The apostles proclaimed the message so that they would have fellowship with the apostles and

---

[12] Marshall, *Epistles of John*, 105.

[13] Ibid., 104.

[14] Stott, *Letters of John*, 67.

[15] Kruse, *Letters of John*, 58.

[16] Carson and Moo, *Introduction to the New Testament*, 685.

therefore with God the Father and his Son. Fellowship with God is bound with fellowship with "us," i.e., the apostles. For us, the apostolic authority is found in the New Testament. We must base our fellowship with God on the sure foundation of the Scriptures.

We also see from these verses that history matters. If Christ did not come in the flesh in history, then the message of Christianity is bogus. Christianity is not a blind leap in the dark, but it is a religion grounded in God's work and entrance into history!

> 4 *And we are writing these things so that our joy may be complete.*

John is a pastor and wants to know that his people are not fellowshipping with those who are not in fellowship with the Father and the Son. It brought the apostle joy to know that his people were walking in the truth. Does it bring you joy to know your fellow believers are walking in the truth? It should. When you hear fellow church members praying Scripture or applying doctrine to their lives, this should warm your heart so that you give thanks to God. I. Howard Marshall writes, "He has the heart of a pastor which cannot be completely happy so long as some of those for whom he feels responsible are not experiencing the full blessings of the gospel."[17] We see the same attitude in 2 and 3 John:

> 2 John 1:4—*I rejoiced greatly to find some of your children walking in the truth, just as we were commanded by the Father.*

> 3 John 1:4—*I have no greater joy than to hear that my children are walking in the truth.*

---

[17] Marshall, *Epistles of John*, 105.

As John Stott nicely summarizes, "This is the divine order—*angelia, koinōnia, chara*"(message, fellowship, joy).[18]

---

[18] Stott, *Letters of John*, 70.

Chapter 3

1 John 1:5-2:2

This is the message we have heard from him and proclaim to you, that God is light, and in him is no darkness at all. If we say we have fellowship with him while we walk in darkness, we lie and do not practice the truth. But if we walk in the light, as he is in the light, we have fellowship with one another, and the blood of Jesus his Son cleanses us from all sin. If we say we have no sin, we deceive ourselves, and the truth is not in us. If we confess our sins, he is faithful and just to forgive us our sins and to cleanse us from all unrighteousness. If we say we have not sinned, we make him a liar, and his word is not in us. My little children, I am writing these things to you so that you may not sin. But if anyone does sin, we have an advocate with the Father, Jesus Christ the righteous. He is the propitiation for our sins, and not for ours only but also for the sins of the whole world.

5 *This is the message we have heard from him and proclaim to you, that God is light, and in him is no darkness at all.*

The message of the apostles is the message given by Jesus. Their message comes from the earthly Jesus. God is light and in him there is no darkness *at all.*[1] John makes a claim about the character of God and will go on to apply his character to our calling to reflect his character. Light and darkness in John are clearly moral categories:[2]

---

[1] Rigidly literal: God is light and darkness in him is not none.

[2] D.A. Carson, *John*, PNTC (Grand Rapids: Eerdmans, 1991), 186; Stott, *Letters of John*, 75-78.

1 John 2:8—*At the same time, it is a new commandment that I am writing to you, which is true in him and in you, because the darkness is passing away and the true light is already shining.*

1 John 2:9—*Whoever says he is in the light and hates his brother is still in darkness.*

1 John 2:11—*But whoever hates his brother is in the darkness and walks in the darkness, and does not know where he is going, because the darkness has blinded his eyes.*

John 1:5—*The light shines in the darkness, and the darkness has not overcome it.*

John 3:19-21—*And this is the judgment: the light has come into the world, and people loved the darkness rather than the light because their works were evil. For everyone who does wicked things hates the light and does not come to the light, lest his works should be exposed. But whoever does what is true comes to the light, so that it may be clearly seen that his works have been carried out in God.*

John 8:12—*I am the light of the world. Whoever follows me will not walk in darkness, but will have the light of life.*

John 9:4-5—*We must work the works of him who sent me while it is day; night is coming, when no one can work. As long as I am in the world, I am the light of the world.*

John 11:10—*But if anyone walks in the night, he stumbles, because the light is not in him.*

John 13:30—*So, after receiving the morsel of bread, he [i.e., Judas] immediately went out. And it was night.*

God's character is absolute moral perfection. So those who claim to know him cannot be indifferent to morality. Light and darkness are ethical terms.

Stott writes, "It is his nature to reveal himself, as it is the property of light to shine; and the revelation is of perfect purity and unutterable majesty."[3] Isaiah 57:15 says, "*For thus says the One who is high and lifted up, who inhabits eternity, whose name is Holy: 'I dwell in the high and holy place, and also with him who is of a contrite and lowly spirit, to revive the spirit of the lowly, and to revive the heart of the contrite.'*" He alone is high and lifted up.

> 6 *If we say we have fellowship with him while we walk in darkness, we lie and do not practice the truth.*

The false teachers so elevated the "spiritual" that they believed they were beyond the realm in which the morality of the body mattered. They mistakenly thought they could have communion with God without walking in the light. They thought one could have spirituality without ethics, but belief and ethics are bound together in the Christian worldview. The *evangel* brings with it an *ethic*.[4]

Of course, in a sense, we all live in darkness. We still live during this present evil age. I. Howard Marshall gives a helpful analogy in this regard. Christians live in the darkness like an actor walking on a dark stage in the circle of light cast by a spotlight which is focused on him.[5] We still live during the era of this present evil age (Gal. 1:4), but we have been given the end-time gift of the Spirit to help navigate our path.

What does it mean to practice (literally *do*) the truth? John helps us out with the following verses from his gospel: "*For everyone who does wicked things hates the light and does not come*

---

[3] Stott, *Letters of John*, 75.

[4] E.g. in Galatians, Paul teaches that the truth of the gospel is to be *obeyed* (see 5:7, with allusions to 2:5 and 2:14). Peter did not obey the gospel.

[5] Marshall, *Epistles of John*, 110.

to the light, lest his works should be exposed. But whoever does what is true comes to the light, so that it may be clearly seen that his works have been carried out in God" (John 3:20-21).[6]

Marshall writes, "The truth is the ultimate reality of God revealed in Jesus and in the Christian message, and that this reality is moral in quality. To practice the truth means to live according to the way revealed by God and so as those who belong to the divine sphere."[7] Christians must take obedience seriously. We must practice what we preach. It is not enough to simply confess.

> 7 *But if we walk in the light, as he is in the light, we have fellowship with one another, and the blood of Jesus his Son cleanses us from all sin.*

Believers are called to walk in the light as God is in the light. This sounds similar to the familiar call to be holy as the Lord is holy. Leviticus 11:44-45 says, *"For I am the LORD your God. Consecrate yourselves therefore, and be holy, for I am holy. You shall not defile yourselves with any swarming thing that crawls on the ground. For I am the LORD who brought you up out of the land of Egypt to be your God. You shall therefore be holy, for I am holy."* Peter quotes this passage in 1 Peter 1:14-16: *"As obedient children, do not be conformed to the passions of your former ignorance, but as he who called you is holy, you also be holy in all your conduct, since it is written, 'You shall be holy, for I am holy.'"* Christians are to be godly, which is short for Godlike. We must walk in the light as he is in the light.

You would think John would say that we have fellowship with God when we walk in the light, but instead he says we

---

[6] Kruse, *Letters of John*, 63.

[7] Marshall, *Epistles of John*, 111.

will have fellowship with *one another*. As Kruse writes, "There is no real fellowship with God which is not expressed in fellowship with other believers."[8] The New Testament voice is uniform in regard to this great truth: vertical love is bound up with horizontal love.

Once again we gain insight into what it means to walk in light or darkness by looking at John's gospel: *"And this is the judgment: the light has come into the world, and people loved the darkness rather than the light because their works were evil. For everyone who does wicked things hates the light and does not come to the light, lest his works should be exposed. But whoever does what is true comes to the light, so that it may be clearly seen that his works have been carried out in God"* (John 3:19-21).[9] To walk in darkness is to do wicked things. To walk in the light is to do what is true.

Another result of walking in the light is that the blood of Jesus cleanses us from all sin. Unpopular though it may be, Christianity is a *bloody* religion. This doesn't appeal to postmodern people, but it must be stated in the clearest terms that to remove blood from Christianity is to pull the plug on biblical religion. Blood is a sacrificial term and is used often to indicate the death of Jesus:[10]

> Mark 14:24—*And he said to them, "This is my blood of the covenant, which is poured out for many."*

---

[8] Kruse, *Letters of John*, 64.

[9] Ibid., 63.

[10] See Leon Morris, *The Apostolic Preaching of the Cross* (Grand Rapids: Eerdmans, 1965), 112-28.

Acts 20:28—*Pay careful attention to yourselves and to all the flock, in which the Holy Spirit has made you overseers, to care for the church of God, which he obtained with his own blood.*

Romans 3:25—*Whom God put forward as a propitiation by his blood, to be received by faith.*

Romans 5:9—*Since, therefore, we have now been justified by his blood, much more shall we be saved by him from the wrath of God.*

Revelation 1:5—*And from Jesus Christ the faithful witness, the firstborn of the dead, and the ruler of kings on earth. To him who loves us and has freed us from our sins by his blood.*

Jesus' blood cleanses us from all sin. Cleansing is tied to forgiveness (1 John 1:9).[11] Jeremiah 33:8 says, *"I will cleanse them from all the guilt of their sin against me, and I will forgive all the guilt of their sin and rebellion against me."*[12]

The verbs for *walk* and *cleanse* are in the present tense showing they are both ongoing activities.[13] They characterize the whole of the Christian life. We are called to reflect God, who is light, by walking in the light. We are called to be Godly, which is a shorthand way of saying we are to be God-like. We must be people of the Book to walk in the light. How else will we know what walking in the light means?

8-10 *If we say we have no sin, we deceive ourselves, and the truth is not in us. If we confess our sins, he is faithful and just to forgive us our sins and to cleanse us from all unrighteousness. If we say we have not sinned, we make him a liar, and his word is not in us.*

---

[11] Graham Cole, *God the Peacemaker* (Downers Grove, IL: IVP, 2009), 164.

[12] Kruse, *Letters of John,* 65.

[13] Ibid., 64.

To claim to be without sin is heretical. It puts one outside the scope of classic Christianity and outside the realm in which salvation can be found. Confession of sin is to be a regular part of our lives.[14]

We must not walk in darkness, and part of not walking in darkness is admitting that we sin. Isn't that interesting? This only makes sense within a Christian understanding of life. Part of not walking in darkness is admitting that at times we walk in darkness. Walking in the light involves confessing our sin regularly. Wolfgang Schrage writes, "Here we have an obvious paradox, which is cited with good reason as the scriptural basis for Luther's *simul iustus simul peccator:* Christians are both righteous and sinful, and therefore need to be forgiven every day."[15]

Similarly, Richard Hays writes, "The distinguishing mark of the community is not so much sinlessness as the willingness to bring their sins into the light, to confess them, and to receive forgiveness and cleansing by the blood of Jesus (1 John 1:5-9). If Jesus is *the Lamb of God who takes away the sin of the world*" (John 1:29), then the church must be the community of those who know themselves to be forgiven sinners. Indeed, those who claim to be sinless are liars (1 John 1:10). Thus, the puzzling passage in 3:4-10 is best read as polemic against the secessionist opponents, who may be claiming to be "born of God" while committing flagrant sin."[16]

---

[14] Kruse writes, "He portrays authentic Christian living as involving honest and ongoing acknowledgement of one's sins," *Letters of John,* 68.

[15] Schrage, *The Ethics of the New Testament,* 312.

[16] Hays, *The Moral Vision of the New Testament,* 155.

This forgiveness and cleansing is a result of confessing. We must be continually confessing sin, all day long. Listen to David confessing his sin before the Lord of hosts:

"Blessed is the one whose transgression is forgiven, whose sin is covered. Blessed is the man against whom the LORD counts no iniquity, and in whose spirit there is no deceit. For when I kept silent, my bones wasted away through my groaning all day long. For day and night your hand was heavy upon me; my strength was dried up as by the heat of summer. Selah I acknowledged my sin to you, and I did not cover my iniquity; I said, 'I will confess my transgressions to the LORD,' and you forgave the iniquity of my sin." (Psalm 32:1-5)

"Have mercy on me, O God, according to your steadfast love; according to your abundant mercy blot out my transgressions. Wash me thoroughly from my iniquity, and cleanse me from my sin!" (Psalm 51:1-2)

It is a great comfort for the sinner to know that as he confesses, God is faithful and just to forgive us our sins and to cleanse us from all unrighteousness. God is faithful. John probably means that God is faithful to his promises. In the great new covenant passage of Jeremiah, we hear, *"For I will forgive their iniquity and I will remember their sin no more"* (Jer. 31:34).

God is faithful *and just.* How can the God who is light dwell with and show favor to those who have and still occasionally walk in darkness and remain just? This is a question many American Christians have never thought about. People just assume God loves them and will forgive them. "That's his job, right?" Wrong. The cross of Christ was not all about us. Without the cross, God's character could be called into question. I mean, have you read the Old Testament? Have you read about the things the people of God did? Even the leaders! David, the man after God's heart, was an adulterer and a murderer. How can God be holy, yet wipe sin under the rug? The answer is that he *does not* wipe sin under the rug. Far from it!

God takes sin so seriously that he sent his one and only Son to pay the penalty we so deserved. This is what Romans 3:21-26 is all about:

> But now the righteousness of God has been manifested apart from the law, although the Law and the Prophets bear witness to it—the righteousness of God through faith in Jesus Christ for all who believe. For there is no distinction: for all have sinned and fall short of the glory of God, and are justified by his grace as a gift, through the redemption that is in Christ Jesus, whom God put forward as a propitiation by his blood, to be received by faith. This was to show God's righteousness, because in his divine forbearance he had passed over former sins. It was to show his righteousness at the present time, so that he might be just and the justifier of the one who has faith in Jesus.

Here we see the inner logic of the cross. We see that the cross has a Godward focus as well as a human one. In the cross, the love of God and justice of God kiss.[17] Yes, God loves us but he also loves his own glory and takes his holiness very seriously.[18] The Father put the Son forward as a propitiation to demonstrate that God is righteous. John will use the language of propitiation in 1 John 2:2 and 4:10.

There is none like our God. He is faithful and just. Exodus 34:5-7 contains a foundational statement about God. It is the nearest thing we have to a systematic statement of the being

---

[17] See the helpful booklet by D. M. Lloyd-Jones, *The Cross: The Vindication of God* (Carlisle, PA: The Banner of Truth Trust, 1999).

[18] See John Piper, *God's Passion for His Glory* (Wheaton, IL: Crossway, 1998).

and attributes of God found in Scripture. Remember, Israel has just prevailed upon Aaron to provide a god to worship while Moses was on the mountain receiving the law. They commit idolatry while still at the bottom of the mountain of God, which is akin to committing adultery on one's wedding night.[19] In turn, the Lord had in effect withdrawn his presence from his people, but Moses pleaded with the Lord and the Lord promised that his presence would go with them (Exod. 33:14-17). The passage reads,

> *The LORD descended in the cloud and stood with him there, and proclaimed the name of the LORD. The LORD passed before him and proclaimed, "The LORD, the LORD, a God merciful and gracious, slow to anger, and abounding in steadfast love and faithfulness, keeping steadfast love for thousands, forgiving iniquity and transgression and sin, but who will by no means clear the guilty, visiting the iniquity of the fathers on the children and the children's children, to the third and the fourth generation."*

Notice that the text does not say, "The Lord, the Lord, a God angry and slow to be merciful and gracious."[20] Yahweh is merciful, gracious, and slow to anger but will by no means clear the guilty. He is faithful and just. What is the only appropriate response to this utterly unique God? *"Moses quickly bowed his head towards the earth and worshipped"* (v. 8).

---

[19] R.W.L. Moberly, "Exodus, Book of," in *Dictionary for Theological Interpretation of the Bible,* ed. Kevin J. Vanhoozer (Grand Rapids: Baker, 2005), 214, quoted in Graham Cole, "Exodus 34, the Middoth and the Doctrine of God: The Importance of Biblical Theology to Evangelical Systematic Theology," *SBJT* 12.3 (Fall 2003), 27.

[20] Cole, *God the Peacemaker,* 74.

This vision of God was fundamental to the prophets.[21] Micah 7:18-20 says, *"Who is a God like you, pardoning iniquity and passing over transgression for the remnant of his inheritance? He does not retain his anger forever, because he delights in steadfast love. He will again have compassion on us; he will tread our iniquities underfoot. You will cast all our sins into the depths of the sea. You will show faithfulness to Jacob and steadfast love to Abraham, as you have sworn to our fathers from the days of old."*

This vision of God was also fundamental to John. He is probably alluding to this passage in his gospel in the following verses:

John 1:14—*And the Word became flesh and dwelt among us, and we have seen his glory, glory as of the only Son from the Father, full of grace and truth.*

John 1:17—*For the law was given through Moses; grace and truth came through Jesus Christ.*

Grace and truth probably harks back to the phrase *loving-kindness* and *truth* (*hesed* and *emet*) in Exodus 34.[22] God is *faithful* to forgive because he has promised to do so and *just* because his Son died for our sins.[23]

If we say we have no sin, we are liars, and we make God a liar and show that his Word has no place in us (1 John

---

[21] The following texts allude to this foundational self-revelation: Num. 14:18, Neh. 9:17, Ps. 103:8, 17, 145:8, Jer. 32:18-19, Joel 2:13, Jonah 4:2; cf. Deut. 5:9-10, 1 Kin. 3:6, Lam. 3:32, Dan. 9:4, Nah. 1:3.

[22] Graham Cole, "Exodus 34," 31; So also Carson, *John*, 129, who writes, "The glory revealed to Moses when the Lord passed in front of him and sounded his name, displaying that divine goodness characterized by ineffable grace and truth, was the very same glory John and his friends saw in the Word-made-flesh."

[23] Stott, *Letters of John*, 82-23.

1:10). This is because the Word teaches the universality of sin in every chapter. Biblical religion is preoccupied with sin:

> 1 Kings 8:46—*If they sin against you—for there is no one who does not sin—and you are angry with them and give them to an enemy, so that they are carried away captive to the land of the enemy, far off or near...*
>
> Psalm 14:3—*They have all turned aside; together they have become corrupt; there is none who does good, not even one.*
>
> Job 15:14—*What is man, that he can be pure? Or he who is born of a woman, that he can be righteous?*
>
> Jer. 17:9—*The heart is deceitful above all things, and desperately sick; who can understand it?*
>
> Prov. 20:9—*Who can say, "I have made my heart pure; I am clean from my sin"?*
>
> Ecc. 7:20—*Surely there is not a righteous man on earth who does good and never sins.*
>
> Isa. 53:6—*All we like sheep have gone astray; we have turned—every one—to his own way; and the LORD has laid on him the iniquity of us all.*
>
> Isa. 64:6—*We have all become like one who is unclean, and all our righteous deeds are like a polluted garment. We all fade like a leaf, and our iniquities, like the wind, take us away.*
>
> Rom. 3:23—*For all have sinned and fall short of the glory of God.*

Without knowledge of sin, the gospel makes no sense.

Before we move to application, notice the parallel between verses 8 and 10 of 1 John 1. If we say we have no sin, we deceive ourselves (v. 8), we make him a liar (v. 10), and the truth is not in us (v. 8) and his word in not in us (v. 10).

We see from these verses that confession of sin must be a regular occurrence, even daily occurrence in the Christian life. The first of Martin Luther's Ninety-Five Theses was on this very point: "When our Lord and Master Jesus Christ said, 'Repent,' he willed the entire life of believers to be one of repentance."[24]

Why must we confess sin if I am already forgiven? For one, the Lord commanded us to: "*Forgive us our debts as we also have forgiven our debtors*" (Matt. 6:12). It is important to properly understand the command to confess though. We are justified once for all. In justification, we are forgiven of all sins past, present, and future from God's perspective. We have confidence that there is no condemnation for those in Christ (Rom. 8:1). But we must appropriate the benefits of justification anew each time we sin. We are not justified again each time. We walk daily in faith with renewed application of the precious gift of righteousness. Christ is our confidence. The Christian comes back to meet God at the cross over and over again. By fresh acts of faith in the message of the cross, we are renewed and we are motivated to maintain our relationship with the Lord. As we take our sin to the cross and take Christ for our righteousness again and again, we are having communion with our King. God takes delight in our frequent appropriations of Christ for our righteousness. God meets us at the cross when we deal with sin his way. He is honored, and we are forgiven and renewed.

We should confess our sins to God and to one another. In his very helpful marriage book, Paul Tripp gives eight reasons showing that the act of confession of sin is a grace from God. It is a grace to:

---

[24] Martin Luther, "Ninety-Five Theses," in *Martin Luther's Basic Theological Writings*, ed. Timothy F. Lull (Minneapolis: Fortress, 1989), 21.

1. Know right from wrong
2. Understand the concept of indwelling sin (we—not something external—are the problem)
3. Have a properly functioning conscience
4. Be protected from self-righteousness
5. See ourselves with accuracy
6. Listen and consider criticism and rebuke
7. Not to be paralyzed by regret
8. Know that we can face our wrongs because Christ has carried our guilt and shame.[25]

Tripp also lists the needed daily habits of a "confession lifestyle": Be lovingly honest, be humble when exposed, do not excuse, be quick to admit wrongs, listen and examine, greet confession with encouragement, be patient, persevering, and gentle in the face of wrong, do not return to the past, and always put your hope in Christ.[26]

In these verses, John gives us two ways to live: a life of continual confession of sin or a life of lying. Believers are called to a lifestyle of light, which consists of walking in the light and regularly confessing sin when we do not.

> 2:1 *My little children, I am writing these things to you so that you may not sin. But if anyone does sin, we have an advocate with the Father, Jesus Christ the righteous.*

John addresses his readers as his *little children*. He is writing with affection to his people with a pastor's heart. John says he is writing *so that* his readers may not sin. So we as

---

[25] Paul David Tripp, *What Did You Expect?* (Wheaton, IL: Crossway, 2010), 73-80.

[26] Ibid., 80-83.

Christians are aided in our fight against sin by the content of this letter. This reality should cause us to heed its contents all the more! John has already said that we are liars if we say we have not sinned, so he knows we will. He says, *"But if anyone does sin, we have an advocate with the Father, Jesus Christ the Righteous One."* Notice the balance here: he is writing so they won't sin; but if anyone does sin, he writes, we have an advocate. He has a realistic view of people.

We have an advocate (*paraklētos*) with the Father. We have one who advocates for us. God is light and we are darkness, and we cannot come to the Father without a mediator. The word for advocate comes from two words: *para* meaning "alongside" and *kaleō* meaning "to call." It is a cognate of the verb *parakaleō* which is translated as "summon, call in, exhort, encourage, or comfort." So a *paraclete* (advocate) is one who is called to one's aid or defense.[27] The NIV says "one who speaks to the Father in our defense." I. Howard Marshall writes, "In present context the word undoubtedly signifies an 'advocate' or 'counsel for the defense' in a legal context. It means a person who intercedes on behalf of somebody else."[28]

In the gospel of John, Jesus used this word to refer to the Holy Spirit (John 14:16, 26, 15:26, 16:7). The same word can be used to refer to both Jesus and the Spirit because they are both God and have the same purpose and plan. So Paul and Peter can speak of the Spirit *of Christ* (Rom. 8:9, Gal. 4:6, Phil. 1:19, 1 Pet. 1:11). Of course, this does not mean that the Son

---

[27] Sinclair Ferguson, *The Holy Spirit* (Downers Grove, IL: IVP, 1996), 36; Stott, *Letters of John,* 85.

[28] Marshall, *Epistles of John,* 116.

and the Spirit are one and the same, but they do the same work. *Functionally*, they are the same. They are "about the same work."[29] There is a unity of purpose among the Father, Son, and Spirit. Sinclair Ferguson writes, "So complete is the union between Jesus and the Paraclete that the coming of the latter is the coming of Jesus himself in the Spirit."[30] Jesus spoke of *another* helper.

Jesus is our advocate; he is at the right hand of the Father right now praying on our behalf. He is our mediator (1 Tim. 2:5). He is our great high priest (Heb. 8:1). Romans 8:34 says, *"Who is to condemn? Christ Jesus is the one who died—more than that, who was raised—who is at the right hand of God, who indeed is interceding for us."* Hebrews 7:25 says, *"Consequently, he is able to save to the uttermost those who draw near to God through him, since he always lives to make intercession for them."*

Our advocate is Jesus Christ the Righteous One. This is a "composite expression indicating his human nature (*Jesus*), messianic office (*Christ*), and righteous character."[31] He was obedient to his Father. The title "Righteous One" is also used in Acts 3:14 and 7:52:

> Acts 3:14—*But you denied the Holy and Righteous One, and asked for a murderer to be granted to you.*

> Acts 7:52—*Which of the prophets did your fathers not persecute? And they killed those who announced beforehand the coming of the Righteous One, whom you have now betrayed and murdered.*

First Peter 3:18 says *"For Christ also suffered once for sins, the righteous for the unrighteous, that he might bring us to God."*

---

[29] Ferguson, *The Holy Spirit*, 54.

[30] Ibid., 56.

[31] Stott, *Letters of John*, 85.

Jesus has no sin of his own and is therefore uniquely qualified to intercede on behalf of his people. He can plead his own righteousness before the Father and ask that his sinful people be forgiven based upon his righteous act (Rom. 5:18).[32] He is our only hope. We are counted righteous because we are united to the Righteous One.

2 He is the propitiation for our sins, and not for ours only but also for the sins of the whole world.

Jesus is both the advocate and the propitiation. "What he pleads on behalf of sinners is what he himself has done on their behalf."[33] Propitiation (*hilasmos*) means a sacrifice that absorbs and removes the wrath of God and turns it to favor.[34] The death of Jesus "was the fulfillment of the Day of Atonement ritual, the most solemn and important rite in Israel's sacrificial system."[35] On that day only the high priest could go behind the curtain that stands in front of the most holy place. He would sprinkle blood on and around the "mercy seat" or "atonement cover" (*hilastērion*) that sat on the top of the ark of the covenant. This mercy seat is the Old Testament background to the word *propitiation*.[36] His was the climactic sacrifice. This is why the temple veil was torn from

---

[32] Marshall, *Epistles of John*, 117. Other references to "righteous" in 1 John show that he is here referring to Jesus' righteous behavior (1:9, 2:29, 3:7, 12).

[33] Ibid., 119.

[34] See Morris, *The Apostolic Preaching of the Cross*, 144-213; John Stott, *The Cross of Christ* (Downers Grove: IVP, 2006), 166-73.

[35] Thielman, *Theology of the New Testament*, 549.

[36] See Lev. 16:6-17. Twenty-one of the 27 occurrences of the word in the OT refer to the mercy seat. See Douglas Moo, *Romans* NICNT (Grand Rapids: Eerdmans, 1996), 232.

top to bottom when Jesus died (Matt. 27:51, Mark 15:38, Luke 23:45). He fulfills the old covenant sacrificial system. Notice all the sacrificial language John uses: blood, cleansing, forgiveness, and propitiation. He is the ultimate mercy seat; he is the new covenant counterpart to the mercy seat; he is the antitype. Atonement is finally found in him!

John Stott writes, "Thus, the Father's provision for the sinning Christian is in his Son, who possesses a threefold qualification: his righteous character, his propitiatory death, and his heavenly advocacy."[37]

As you may be aware, there is a lot of debate about this phrase. Why do you think that is? People don't like a God of wrath. This is why there is also intense debate even within "evangelicalism" concerning penal substitution.[38] The Scriptures seem clear, but people do not want a Holy God who punishes sin. The problem with denying this aspect of God is the Bible.[39] God is holy, so there must be wrath. Wrath is the response of a holy God to sin. As Carson writes, "In

---

[37] Stott, *Letters of John,* 88.

[38] Penal substitution is the view that Christ paid the penalty (hence penal) that our sins (hence substitution) deserved. In my opinion, one cannot deny this and remain an evangelical.

[39] For a robust defense of penal substitution biblically, pastorally, historically, and polemically, see Steve Jeffery, Michale Ovey, and Andrew Sach, *Pierced for Our Transgressions* (Wheaton: Crossway, 2007); also see Thomas R. Schreiner's entry in *The Nature of the Atonement* (Downers Grove: IL, 2006).

Scripture, God's wrath is nothing other than his holiness when it confronts the rebellion of his creatures."[40]

Some scholars who do not want to attribute wrath to God argue that the word does not mean propitiation, but expiation, which is the removal of sin and guilt. As is often the case, there is no need for an either/or interpretation here though.[41] This word can communicate both senses. As Robert Letham writes, "The question of propitiating is realized when it is asked who requires expiation for our sins."[42] The Old Testament frequently connects the removal of sin (expiation) or forgiving with the removal of God's wrath (propitiation).

Some have distorted and misrepresented this biblical teaching. For example, Steve Chalke writes, "How then, have we come to believe that at the cross this God of love suddenly decides to vent his anger and wrath on his own Son? The fact is that the cross isn't a form of cosmic child abuse—a vengeful Father, punishing his Son for an offence he has not even committed."[43] What are we to make of this? Does 1 John (or the rest of the New Testament for that matter) teach divine child abuse? Is God an angry Father? Absolutely not. This is a caricature that results from not reading the Bible. The aversion to the wrath of God among contem-

---

[40] D.A. Carson, "Atonement in Romans 3:21-26," in *The Glory of the Atonement*, ed. Charles E. Hill and Frank A. James III (Downers Grove, IL: IVP, 2004), 131-32.

[41] Cole, *God the Peacemaker*, 146; Marshall, *Epistles of John*, 118.

[42] Robert Letham, *The Work of Christ* (Downers Grove, IL: IVP, 1993), 141.

[43] Steve Chalke, *The Lost Message of Jesus* (Grand Rapids: Zondervan, 2003), 182.

porary Christians is in part due to their aversion of the Holy Scriptures. This act of putting forth Christ as a propitiation for our sins is God's *loving* initiative. The *Father* is the one who is faithful and just to forgive sins. His love results in propitiation. We see this in 1 John: *"In this is love, not that we have loved God but that he loved us and sent his Son to be the propitiation for our sins"* (4:10). One who thinks that Christ's propitiatory self-sacrifice is child abuse does not truly know the love of God and misunderstands the heart of the gospel.

John says that Christ was the propitiation for our sins, but not for ours only but also for the sins of the whole world. Here we run up against the historic in-house debate over God's sovereignty that in some ways stretches back to the 4th century with Augustine and Pelagius. After the Protestant Reformation, this debate has been known as Calvinism versus Arminianism. I am a five-point Calvinist and want to take some time to show why this verse does not contradict what has historically been called "limited atonement."

First, let's appreciate the Arminian interpretation. It says *world*! They are taking the Bible seriously. All too often, Calvinists become arrogant and self-righteous. They snub their noses at those "inferior Arminians."[44] This is ridiculous. Arminians are our brothers and sisters in Christ. Calvinists must remember that the same God that is meticulously sovereign over the extent of the atonement is also sovereign over theological understanding. We have nothing, including doctrinal precision that we have not received. So this debate should be characterized by love and humility. Arminians are

---

[44] I recall seeing a sticker that read "Calvinism: What happens when Arminians read the Bible."

seeking to be faithful to the Scriptures. This verse says Christ was the propitiation for the sins of the whole world, and they want to take John, and God, at his Word. But we must ask how the Scriptures use the word *world*. We will examine this below.

Let's also admit that *all* Christians "limit" the atonement in some way. Arminians limit the effectiveness of the cross while Calvinists limit the extent. I prefer to call it "definite atonement" since no one likes to limit the work of Jesus.

I recall hearing Dr. D. James Kennedy illustrate how the Bible uses universal language when the referent is not absolutely universal: universal terms often refer to a limited group. For instance, in a class the professor will say, "Is everyone here today?" He doesn't mean every single person in the whole world. We all say "all," all the time. No, we don't; some speak other languages and never use the word "all." You say "all," all the time. No, you don't; sometimes you sleep. Universal terms are used everywhere. Wait, no, they're not. Not everywhere. We use them this way all the time. No, we don't. If I were to stop you every time you used a universal term, I'd be stopping you all the time; well, no, I wouldn't, not *all* the time. You get the point.

First John 2:2 says Jesus was the propitiation for the whole world. We must ask what John meant by *world* (*kosmos*) here. First John alone uses the word 23 times. John uses the word 78 times in his gospel, all with a range of meanings depending on context.[45] Let us examine some of these uses to see that an appeal to this word does not settle the debate:

---

[45] Kruse, *Letters of John*, 74.

John 1:10—*He was in the world, and the world was made through him, yet the world did not know him.* World cannot mean every single person in the world here for many did know him.

John 7:7—*The world cannot hate you, but it hates me because I testify about it that its works are evil.* Here, the world cannot refer to every single person because the world hates Jesus. Many love Jesus.

John 12:19—*So the Pharisees said to one another, "You see that you are gaining nothing. Look, the world has gone after him."* Did every single person in the world go after him?

John 15:18—*If the world hates you, know that it has hated me before it hated you.*

1 John 2:15—*Do not love the world or the things in the world. If anyone loves the world, the love of the Father is not in him.* If the world is every single person, then we should not love other Christians according to this verse.

1 John 3:1—*See what kind of love the Father has given to us, that we should be called children of God; and so we are. The reason why the world does not know us is that it did not know him.*

1 John 3:13—*Do not be surprised, brothers, that the world hates you.*

1 John 4:5—*They are from the world; therefore they speak from the world, and the world listens to them.*

1 John 5:19—*We know that we are from God, and the whole world lies in the power of the evil one.* Clearly, Christians do not lie in the power of the evil one.

Revelation 12:9—*And the great dragon was thrown down, that ancient serpent, who is called the devil and Satan, the deceiver of the whole world—he was thrown down to the earth, and his angels were thrown down with him.*

Paul uses the word in a similar fashion:

Romans 1:8—*First, I thank my God through Jesus Christ for all of you, because your faith is proclaimed in all the world.*

Romans 11:12—*Now if their trespass means riches for the world, and if their failure means riches for the Gentiles, how much more will their full inclusion mean!* Here Paul equates world with Gentiles.

Colossians 1:5-6—*Because of the hope laid up for you in heaven. Of this you have heard before in the word of the truth, the gospel, which has come to you, as indeed in the whole world it is bearing fruit and growing—as it also does among you, since the day you heard it and understood the grace of God in truth...*

More passages could be cited, but this should be sufficient to show that the claim that "the verse says *world*" does not automatically show the Calvinist view is a misreading.

John was writing primarily to a Jewish audience. We know this from the constant emphasis on the fact that they had seen, heard, and touched the Jewish Messiah. Also, Galatians 2:9 reads, *"And when James and Cephas and John, who seemed to be pillars, perceived the grace that was given to me, they gave the right hand of fellowship to Barnabas and me, that we should go to the Gentiles and they to the circumcised."* John, unlike Paul, was primarily an apostle to the circumcised (i.e., the Jews).

A very important passage that helps us understand 1 John 2:2 is John 11:51-52.[46] That passage says, *"He did not say this of his own accord, but being high priest that year he prophesied that Jesus would die for the nation, and not for the nation only, but also to gather into one the children of God who are scattered abroad."* Notice the parallel between the verses:

---

[46] John Owen, *The Death of Death* (Edinburgh: The Banner of Truth, 2002), 225.

John 11:51-52:

A—Jesus would die for the nation

B—And not for the nation only,

C—But also

D—To gather the children of God who are scattered abroad.

1 John 2:2:

A'—He is the propitiation for our sins,

B'—And not for ours only

C'—But also

D'—For the sins of the whole world.

We see from these verses from John that *world* in 1 John 2:2 is equivalent to "the children of God who are scattered abroad" in John 11. In other words, John is telling the Jewish disciples that Christ is the Savior of the world (John 1:29), not simply the Savior of the Jews.

Furthermore, John would not have needed to throw in the word *also* if he meant for the term *world* to mean every single person. He wrote, "*Not for ours only **but also** for the sins of the whole world.*"[47] If *world* meant every single person, there would be no need for any distinction between *ours* and *world*. John could have just said "whole world."

Some say he died for all, but the cross only becomes effective when a person believes; but as John Owen has asked, is unbelief not sin? First John 3:23 *commands* us to believe in Christ. Unbelief is disobedience to this command (cf. Rev. 21:8). If unbelief is not sin and all of their sins have been

---

[47] A.W. Pink, *The Sovereignty of God* (Baker Books, 1984), 259-60.

paid for, then why should they be punished for unbelief? If all of their sins are paid for except for rejecting Christ, and if it is not a sin, how can they be punished for it? And what about those who never hear the gospel and don't have a chance to reject Christ? How can they be punished if all of their sins are paid for? If it is sin (and, of course, rejecting Christ is a sin, as we have seen), then Christ underwent the punishment due for it, and they cannot be cast into hell.

Others say Christ died for all without distinction but the cross only becomes effective when we are united to Christ; however, Ephesians 1:3 says the elect were united to Christ in eternity past. We were chosen *in Christ* before the foundation of the world.

Another problem with interpreting *world* as every single person is the issue of double payment. As we have seen, propitiation is a sacrifice that absorbs God's wrath and turns it to favor. If God's wrath has been extinguished on the cross for all people, then how could there be a place called hell? There would be no wrath for God to express. If Christ paid the penalty for John Doe on the cross and absorbed the wrath that John Doe deserved, then how could God punish him again? He was already punished in Christ at the cross.

Yet another issue to keep in mind is the link between Christ as our advocate and our propitiation. Intercession and atonement are bound together. This is illustrated by the high priest who had 12 stones on his chest to represent the 12 tribes of Israel. The priest was not representing Babylon or Assyria, but Israel. So in the new covenant, the priest represents the elect. John 17:6-9 says, *"I have manifested your name to the people whom you gave me out of the world. Yours they were, and you gave them to me, and they have kept your word.*

Now they know that everything that you have given me is from you. For I have given them the words that you gave me, and they have received them and have come to know in truth that I came from you; and they have believed that you sent me. I am praying for them. I am not praying for the world but for those whom you have given me, for they are yours." Jesus does not pray for the world. Jesus only prays for the elect (those the Father has given him). Jesus intercedes for and atones for the elect alone.

There is Trinitarian harmony in the work of salvation. The Father elects, the Son redeems, and the Spirit calls. The Son only redeems those given to him, and the Spirit only opens the eyes of those for whom Christ died. I recently heard a rap song by Shai Linne called "Mission Accomplished" that lays it out quite nicely:

Here's a controversial subject that tends to divide
For years it's had Christians lining up on both sides
By God's grace, I'll address this without pride
The question concerns those for whom Christ died
Was He trying to save everybody worldwide?
Was He trying to make the entire world His Bride?
Does man's unbelief keep the Savior's hands tied?
Biblically, each of these must be denied
It's true, Jesus gave up His life for His Bride
But His Bride is the elect, to whom His death is applied
If on judgment day, you see that you can't hide
And because of your sin, God's wrath on you abides
And hell is the place you eternally reside
That means your wrath from God hasn't been satisfied
But we believe His mission was accomplished when He died

Father, Son and Spirit: three and yet one
Working as a unit to get things done

Our salvation began in eternity past
God certainly has to bring all His purpose to pass
A triune, eternal bond no one could ever sever
When it comes to the church, peep how they work together
The Father foreknew first, the Son came to earth
To die- the Holy Spirit gives the new birth
The Father elects them, the Son pays their debt and protects
them
The Spirit is the One who resurrects them
The Father chooses them, the Son gets bruised for them
The Spirit renews them and produces fruit in them
Everybody's not elect, the Father decides
And it's only the elect in whom the Spirit resides
The Father and the Spirit- completely unified

My third and final verse- here's the situation
Just a couple more things for your consideration
If saving everybody was why Christ came in history
With so many in hell, we'd have to say He failed miserably
So many think He only came to make it possible
Let's follow this solution to a conclusion that's logical
What about those who were already in the grave?
The Old Testament wicked- condemned as depraved
Did He die for them? C'mon, behave
But worst of all, you're saying the cross by itself doesn't save
That we must do something to give the cross its power
That means, at the end of the day, the glory's ours
That man-centered thinking is not recommended
The cross will save all for whom it was intended
Because for the elect, God's wrath was satisfied[48]

Or in the words of the "Prince of Preachers," Charles
Spurgeon:

---

[48] Shai Linne, *The Atonement* (Lamp Mode Recordings, 2008).

We are often told that we limit the atonement of Christ, because we say that Christ has not made a satisfaction for all
men, or all men would be saved. Now, our reply to this is that,
on the other hand, our opponents limit it: we do not. The Arminians say, "Christ died for all men." Ask them what they
mean by it. Did Christ die so as to secure the salvation of all
men? They say, "No, certainly not." We ask them the next question — Did Christ die so as to secure the salvation of any man
in particular? They answer, "No." They are obliged to admit
this if they are consistent. They say, "No, Christ has died that
any man may be saved if" — and then follow certain conditions
of salvation. We say, then, we will just go back to the old
statement — Christ did not die so as beyond a doubt to secure
the salvation of anybody, did he? You must say, "No;" you are
obliged to say so, for you believe that even after a man has
been pardoned, he may yet fall from grace, and perish. Now,
who is it that limits the death of Christ? Why, you. You say
that Christ did not die so as to infallibly secure the salvation of
anybody. We beg your pardon; when you say we limit Christ's
death, we say, "No, my dear sir, it is you that do it." We say
Christ so died that he infallibly secured the salvation of a mul-
titude that no man can number, who through Christ's death
not only may be saved, but are saved, must be saved, and cannot by any possibility run the hazard of being anything but
saved. You are welcome to your atonement; you may keep it.
We will never renounce ours for the sake of it.[49]

So John is saying that Christ is the propitiation for our
sins, and not for the sins of the Jews only, but also the Gentiles!

[49] Charles Spurgeon quoted in J.I. Packer's "Introductory Essay" in John
Owen, *The Death of Death* (Edinburgh: The Banner of Truth, 2002), 14
n.1.

Chapter 4

1 John 2:3-14

And by this we know that we have come to know him, if we keep his commandments. Whoever says "I know him" but does not keep his commandments is a liar, and the truth is not in him, but whoever keeps his word, in him truly the love of God is perfected. By this we may know that we are in him: whoever says he abides in him ought to walk in the same way in which he walked. Beloved, I am writing you no new commandment, but an old commandment that you had from the beginning. The old commandment is the word that you have heard. At the same time, it is a new commandment that I am writing to you, which is true in him and in you, because the darkness is passing away and the true light is already shining. Whoever says he is in the light and hates his brother is still in darkness. Whoever loves his brother abides in the light, and in him there is no cause for stumbling. But whoever hates his brother is in the darkness and walks in the darkness, and does not know where he is going, because the darkness has blinded his eyes. I am writing to you, little children, because your sins are forgiven for his name's sake. I am writing to you, fathers, because you know him who is from the beginning. I am writing to you, young men, because you have overcome the evil one. I write to you, children, because you know the Father. I write to you, fathers, because you know him who is from the beginning. I write to you, young men, because you are strong, and the word of God abides in you, and you have overcome the evil one.

3-4 *And by this we know that we have come to know him, if we keep his commandments. Whoever says "I know him" but does not keep his commandments is a liar, and the truth is not in him.*

John speaks of "knowing the Lord." This is the universal religious longing. The false teachers thought they knew

God. In the introduction, I mentioned that that particular heresy would evolve into Gnosticism. Gnosticism comes from the word *gnōsis,* which means knowledge. John lays out true knowledge of the true God.

John now applies the first test: obedience. Do the false teachers know the Lord? How do we know that we know the Lord? John's answer is that we know we know him if we keep his commandments. How can you assure your heart? Look at your life! This is probably a drastically different way than you normally think. Many teachers say only look outside of yourself. This is, of course, true, but it is not the whole truth. Robert Murray McCheyne (1813-1843) used to say, "For every one look at ourselves, we should take ten looks at Christ," which again is very true (Heb. 12:2); but according to the apostle John, that one look at ourselves is very important. Now we are not talking about endless naval gazing, but we are called to examine ourselves to see whether we are truly in the faith (2 Cor. 13:5).

Matthew 7:21-23 says, *"Not everyone who says to me, 'Lord, Lord,' will enter the kingdom of heaven, but the one who does the will of my Father who is in heaven. On that day many will say to me, 'Lord, Lord, did we not prophesy in your name, and cast out demons in your name, and do many mighty works in your name?' And then will I declare to them, 'I never knew you; depart from me, you workers of lawlessness.'"* Jesus said he never knew them. That is the issue. If they would have truly known Christ, they would have done the will of the Father.

One who claims to know the Lord but is not obeying his commandments is a liar. I can think of various friends who have so deceived themselves. Consider the woman who "feels led" to leave her husband because her "needs" are not being met. She is being led alright, by the prince of the power of the air. Consider the man who thinks that it is God's will to abandon his wife for a woman he is (temporarily) more sexually attracted to. That is god's will—the will of the god of this age. Such people cannot claim to know the Lord. Consider the teenage believer who enters a dating relationship with an unbeliever. Consider the so-called Christian couple involved in sexual immorality before they are married but think that it's okay because once they marry, they will be "legal." Consider the couple who hoards all they have and refuse to live a generous life. Such people do not truly know the Lord.

It must be asked, "What commandments are John speaking of?" First John uses this word *commandments* 14 times. The fundamental commandment is to believe in the name of Jesus Christ (1 John 3:23), but belief never stays "in the air." If it is to be biblical, it must hit the ground running. We tend to have a Greek view of faith, rather than a Hebrew view. Faith is fundamentally receptive in receiving salvation, but it never stays passive. It gets busy from the beginning. Faith *works* (Gal. 5:6, Rom. 1:5).

There is no hint in this letter, or in any of John's writings, that he is referring to the Mosaic law.[1] The commandments in 1 John are to believe in Jesus and love our fellow Christians as Jesus loved. As Wolfgang Schrage writes, "According to John, Christian duty can be summed up in a single

---

[1] Kruse, *Letters of John*, 79; Schrage writes, "These commandments, however, are no longer identical with those of the Old Testament.... The law no longer plays any role as a guide to conduct," *The Ethics of the New Testament*, 304 (cf. also 305, 306, 308).

phrase: brotherly love.... The commandments are but a single commandment, and this single commandment is the law of love."[2] Jesus said that this is his commandment: to love one another as he has loved us (John 15:12). Though John does not use this terminology, it is theologically safe to say that these commandments refer to the law of Christ. Elsewhere, I have given the following theological definition for the law of Christ as the ethical standard of the new covenant:

1. The law of love

2. The example of Jesus

3. The teaching of Jesus

4. The teaching of the apostles

5. The teaching of the whole canon interpreted in light of the coming of Christ[3]

Obviously, John does not spell all this out. In fact, he doesn't define the commandments for us at all.[4] He assumes his hearers will know what he means.

> 5-6 *but whoever keeps his word, in him truly the love of God is perfected. By this we may know that we are in him: whoever says he abides in him ought to walk in the same way in which he walked.*

Again we see that we must know his commandments if we are to keep them. Christians must order our lives around his Word. Notice the parallel of keeping his commandments in verse 4 and keeping his word in verse 5.

---

[2] Schrage, *The Ethics of the New Testament*, 314.

[3] *The Law of Christ: A Theological Proposal* (Frederick, MD: New Covenant Media, 2010).

[4] Hays, *The Moral Vision of the New Testament*, 138.

This phrase *love of God* is ambiguous. Does John mean God's love for us or our love for God? It could be both love for God and God's love of us, but I lean more towards our love for God (cf. 1 John 2:15, 5:3).[5]

Perfected means that our love is mature. Love is patterned after Christ. It means not looking for personal reward but for the benefit of the others (Phil. 2:2-8). Love is self-giving (Gal. 5:13-14). We are not talking about a mere feeling, but moral obedience. We see this clearly from John's gospel:

John 14:15—*If you love me, you will keep my commandments.*

John 14:21—*Whoever has my commandments and keeps them, he it is who loves me.*

John 14:23—*Jesus answered him, "If anyone loves me, he will keep my word, and my Father will love him, and we will come to him and make our home with him."*

John 15:10—*If you keep my commandments, you will abide in my love, just as I have kept my Father's commandments and abide in his love.*[6]

Jesus is our example. We must live *as he lived*. I. Howard Marshall writes, "The test of our religious experience is whether it produces a reflection of the life of Jesus in our daily life."[7] We must repeatedly ask, "How do we know how he walked?" We must immerse ourselves in the Gospels and seek to learn how to live from our Lord.

---

[5] Marshall, *Epistles of John*, 125.

[6] Stott, *Letters of John*, 95.

[7] Marshall, *Epistles of John*, 128.

When John speaks about living in God, he has in mind
the new and real spiritual communion that we enjoy by the
Spirit in the new covenant.[8]

> 7 *Beloved, I am writing you no new commandment, but an old*
> *commandment that you had from the beginning. The old command-*
> *ment is the word that you have heard.*

Now John applies the third test: love. John is showing
that he is not making up anything new. His teaching is
simply the teaching of Jesus. The commandment is not new,
but goes back to Jesus. It is the commandment that Jesus had
given. His opponents may have accused John of adding
"new commandments" that they did not have to follow, but
John wants to show it is from Jesus himself. In 2 John 5, he
wrote, "*And now I ask you, dear lady — not as though I were writ-*
ing you a new commandment, but the one we have had from the
beginning — that we love one another." In John 15:12, Jesus had
said, "*This is my commandment, that you love one another as I*
have loved you." In John 13:34, Jesus said, "*A new command-*
ment I give to you, that you love one another: just as I have loved
you, you also are to love one another." Jesus' new command
was old for the audience of 1 John. It is what they had heard
from the beginning.

In verses 3 and 4, John spoke of commandments (plural —
entolas), but here he speaks of the commandment (singular —
entolē). The switch from plural to singular is due to the fact
that for John, all the commandments are summed up in one
commandment: mutual love.[9] John Stott writes, "Brotherly
love was part of the original message which had come to

---

[8] Kruse, *Letters of John*, 81.

[9] Marshall, *Epistles of John*, 129; Stott, *Letters of John*, 97.

them. John was not now inventing it. It was not an innova-
tion such as the heretics claimed to teach. It was as old as the
gospel itself."[10]

> 8 *At the same time, it is a new commandment that I am writing to*
> *you, which is true in him and in you, because the darkness is passing*
> *away and the true light is already shining.*

At the same time, it is new. John is showing that even
though Jesus gave the commandment, there is now something new. Jesus has since died, rose again, and poured out
the Spirit. It is one thing to have Jesus tell you to love one
another as he has loved them. It is quite another to have Jesus tangibly show you what love looks like. As Stott writes,
"The idea of love in general was not new, but Jesus Christ
invested it in several ways with a richer and deeper meaning."[11] We are called to walk as he walked (1 John 2:6). Philippians 2:3-11 is one of the greatest passages that shows
how to live in a Christ-like manner:

> *Do nothing from rivalry or conceit, but in humility count others*
> *more significant than yourselves. Let each of you look not only to his*
> *own interests, but also to the interests of others. Have this mind*
> *among yourselves, which is yours in Christ Jesus, who, though he*
> *was in the form of God, did not count equality with God a thing to be*
> *grasped, but made himself nothing, taking the form of a servant, be-*
> *ing born in the likeness of men. And being found in human form, he*
> *humbled himself by becoming obedient to the point of death, even*
> *death on a cross. Therefore God has highly exalted him and bestowed*
> *on him the name that is above every name, so that at the name of Je-*
> *sus every knee should bow, in heaven and on earth and under the*

---

[10] Stott, *Letters of John*, 97.

[11] Stott, *Letters of John*, 97.

earth, and every tongue confess that Jesus Christ is Lord, to the glory of God the Father.

As Wolfgang Schrage notes, "It is also true that 'new' is primarily an eschatological predicate. It appears in such contexts as 'new covenant,' 'new song,' 'new creation,' designating an eschatological quality. The law of love is 'new' because 'the true light is already shining' (1 John 2:8). Love is a sign of realized eschatology, an essential element implicit in the new reality of Christ."[12]

I. Howard Marshall rightly suggests that "*which is true in him and in you*" could be translated, "its fulfillment is seen in him and in you."[13] This command is "truly expressed" in him and in you.[14] John is assuring them that they are bearing fruit.

John also says the darkness is passing away and the true light is already shining. The darkness is the realm in which sinful behavior predominates.[15] This realm is passing away. Paul used this same verb (*paragō*) in 1 Corinthians 7:31 where he wrote, "*the present form of this world is passing away.*" The end of this present evil age is drawing near. In 1 John 2:17, John writes that the "*world is passing away along with its desires.*" Here we have the heart of New Testament eschatology: the already but not yet. The New Testament consistently teaches inaugurated eschatology. The kingdom has come, but not in its fullness. The new age is here, but it overlaps with the old age. Jesus gave himself for our sins to

---

[12] Schrage, *The Ethics of the New Testament,* 315; Stott, *Letters of John,* 98.

[13] Marshall, *The Epistles of John,* 130.

[14] Kruse, *Letters of John,* 83.

[15] Ibid., 84.

deliver us from the present evil age (Gal. 1:4). In Jesus Christ, the future has invaded the present. The end of the ages has come on the church (1 Cor. 10:11). The darkness is passing away, and the true light is already shining.

9-11 Whoever says he is in the light and hates his brother is still in darkness. Whoever loves his brother abides in the light, and in him there is no cause for stumbling. But whoever hates his brother is in the darkness and walks in the darkness, and does not know where he is going, because the darkness has blinded his eyes.

John starts this verse with *"Whoever says"* as he did in previous verses:

- "If we say…" (1 John 1:6)
- "If we say…" (1 John 1:8)
- "If we confess…" (1 John 1:9)
- "If we say…" (1 John 1:10)
- "Whoever says…" (1 John 2:4)
- "Whoever says…" (1 John 2:6)

It is very evident that the false teachers *claimed* a lot of things, but John wants to show his readers (which includes us) that true Christianity consists of much more than simply words. This is a word the church in America needs to hear. There are still many people who *claim* to be Christians. John wants us all to know that a certain way of life must accompany that confession. In this verse, that way of life is characterized by love for fellow Christians.

This new eschatological situation brings with it the call to live by the power of the Spirit as God's end-time people in a world order that is on its way out.[16] The fundamental characteristic of this people is to be love for one another. The light of Jesus Christ is already shining, and the proper behavior of his people who live in that light is love for fellow Christians. If you do not love your fellow Christians, you are still in darkness. You are still living according to the patterns of the old age. But whoever loves his fellow Christian abides in the light. Mutual love shows that they are in Christ and have the Spirit. We are called to lay down our lives in concrete ways for the good of our fellow believers because the light is already shining. As Richard Mouw put it, "By doing these things here and now, we can experience something of the light of God's glory—a light that will someday shine eternally in the Holy City."[17]

Notice John does not say, "Whoever *says* he loves his fellow Christian" in verse ten. He simply says, *"Whoever loves*

---

[16] Gordon Fee, *Paul, the Spirit, and the People of God* (Peabody, MA: Hendrickson, 1996), 51; Marshall writes, "The darkness of the old age, in which men did not love in this sort of way, is disappearing, and the light of the new age, in which Christian love is shown, is already shining. The picture is that of a world in the darkness of night, but the first rays of the dawning sun have already begun to shine; more and more areas are becoming light instead of dark, and the light is getting brighter. There are still dark places, completely sunk in shadow, but there are places where there is bright light, and it is here that the disciples are to be found, walking in the light and themselves shedding light. This is how John expresses the thought of the two overlapping eras of the old and new creations," Marshall, *The Epistles of John*, 130.

[17] Richard Mouw, *When the Kings Come Marching In* (Grand Rapids: Eerdmans, 2002), 130.

his brother." It should be very clear that John is concerned about actions, not words (1 John 3:18).[18]

A person who loves his fellow Christian won't stumble because they are obviously walking by the Spirit. Their priorities are straight. A person who does not love his fellow Christian is lost and in trouble.

How do these verses shape what the Christian life should look like? Too often, we think we are pleasing the Lord when we are avoiding sin, which is, of course, true, but John would say that is an insufficient view of the Christian life. There are sins of commission and sins of omission. For John, true spiritual life is characterized by positive acts of love, not simply avoiding sin.[19] This should cause us to pause and ask ourselves, "What I am *doing* for the benefit of fellow believers?"

12-14 *I am writing to you, little children, because your sins are forgiven for his name's sake. I am writing to you, fathers, because you know him who is from the beginning. I am writing to you, young men, because you have overcome the evil one. I write to you, children, because you know the Father. I write to you, fathers, because you know him who is from the beginning. I write to you, young men, because you are strong, and the word of God abides in you, and you have overcome the evil one.*

John pauses to assure his readers and provide the basis for the following verses (2:15-17).[20] The first three occurrences of *I write* are in the present tense, and the last three are in the aorist tense. John addresses all believers with these titles.

---

[18] Marshall, *The Epistles of John,* 132.

[19] Ibid., 133.

[20] Ibid., 135.

It is a rhetorical device to indicate the qualities that are appropriate to the three stages of life, which should be true of all believers. Every community consists of people of varying maturity. I. Howard Marshall writes, "All Christians should have the innocence of childhood, the strength of youth, and the mature knowledge of age."[21] This wording may seem odd to us, but John is utilizing stylistic variation and repetition for emphasis.

---

[21] Ibid., 138; so also Kruse, *Letters of John*, 88.

Chapter 5

1 John 2:15-27

Do not love the world or the things in the world. If anyone loves the world, the love of the Father is not in him. For all that is in the world—the desires of the flesh and the desires of the eyes and pride in possessions—is not from the Father but is from the world. And the world is passing away along with its desires, but whoever does the will of God abides forever. Children, it is the last hour, and as you have heard that antichrist is coming, so now many antichrists have come. Therefore we know that it is the last hour. They went out from us, but they were not of us; for if they had been of us, they would have continued with us. But they went out, that it might become plain that they all are not of us. But you have been anointed by the Holy One, and you all have knowledge. I write to you, not because you do not know the truth, but because you know it, and because no lie is of the truth. Who is the liar but he who denies that Jesus is the Christ? This is the antichrist, he who denies the Father and the Son. No one who denies the Son has the Father. Whoever confesses the Son has the Father also. Let what you heard from the beginning abide in you. If what you heard from the beginning abides in you, then you too will abide in the Son and in the Father. And this is the promise that he made to us—eternal life. I write these things to you about those who are trying to deceive you. But the anointing that you received from him abides in you, and you have no need that anyone should teach you. But as his anointing teaches you about everything, and is true, and is no lie—just as it has taught you, abide in him.

15 *Do not love the world or the things in the world. If anyone loves the world, the love of the Father is not in him.*

The old cliché is true: Christians are in the world, but not of it. We live in this world but are called not to love it. As

D.L. Moody said, "The ship belongs in the water of the world, but if the water gets in the ship, it sinks." To love the world is to be worldly. Worldliness is disobedience to God's rule of life.[1] Theologian David Wells defines worldliness as "that system of values, in any given age, which has at its center our fallen human perspective, which displaces God and his truth from the world, and which makes sin look normal and righteousness seem strange."[2]

We see from this verse that we are to resist the world. The Bible teaches that there are three forms of evil influence: world, flesh, and the devil. Ephesians 2:1-3 says, *"And you were dead in the trespasses and sins in which you once walked, following the course of this world, following the prince of the power of the air, the spirit that is now at work in the sons of disobedience—among whom we all once lived in the passions of our flesh, carrying out the desires of the body and the mind, and were by nature children of wrath, like the rest of mankind."* Notice that these verses mention all three of our enemies: the course of the world, the prince of the power of the air, and the passions of our flesh. Unbelievers are enslaved to these enemies. Christians are free through the death and resurrection of Christ and the power of the Spirit, but we can still be influenced by them. They remain enemies to be fought.

World in this context refers to societal attitudes, habits, and preferences that are at odds with God's purposes. It is a system organized in opposition to God. It is the social environment in which we live. The world includes all the wicked aspects of culture, peer pressure, values, traditions, customs,

---

[1] Ibid., 143.

[2] David Wells, *Losing Our Virtue* (Grand Rapids: Eerdmans, 1998), 4.

philosophies, and attitudes. Our culture impacts us more deeply than we are aware. Like a fish in water who does not realize it is wet, we are influenced by Godless thinking without even realizing it.

The flesh is the inner drive, or inclination, or propensity of people to do evil (see Gal. 5:16-17).[3] It is who we were in Adam. John has already mentioned that we are capable of deceiving ourselves (1 John 1:8). We cannot blame the world for all of our sin and temptations. We are also the problem.

As Clinton Arnold writes, "The devil is an intelligent, powerful spirit-being that is thoroughly evil and is directly involved in perpetrating evil in the lives of individuals as well as on a much larger scale."[4] The devil is a real enemy. Peter says he prowls around like a roaring lion seeking someone to devour (1 Pet. 5:8). But the devil is not our only problem. It is not "all the devil's fault."

In the news, we often hear psychopaths blaming their evil deeds on the devil: "The devil made me do it." We can't simply blame the devil, or simply our corrupt culture, or simply our own sinfulness. They work together. So if a man cheats on his wife, we know there are several factors. The world constantly elevates sensual pleasure to an unrealistic level. The media makes sexual promiscuity normal. So the world is part of the cause. But the man's own uncontrolled lust is also a major cause. Finally, Satan loves to split marriages and bring destruction because marriage is a picture of

---

[3] Clinton Arnold, *Powers of Darkness*, (Downers Grove, IL: IVP, 1992), 124.

[4] Clinton Arnold, *Three Crucial Questions about Spiritual Warfare* (Grand Rapids: Baker Books, 1997), 35.

the Christ/church relationship, which he abhors. With almost every sinful act, we could point out ways the world,
the flesh, and the devil influenced the act. Clinton Arnold
writes, "The Bible takes all three seriously. The inner inclination to think and do evil (the flesh) and the external pressure
to conform to ungodly social standards (the world) are seen
as just as important as the supernaturally powerful beings
who are hostile to God and his people."[5] But because of the
presence of the empowering presence of God, we can resist.

The *love of the Father* probably refers to our love for the Father rather than the Father's love for us. If we love the
world, we do not love the Father.[6] Love of the world and
love of the Father are incompatible. As James says, *"You
adulterous people! Do you not know that friendship with the world
is enmity with God? Therefore whoever wishes to be a friend of the
world makes himself an enemy of God"* (James 4:4).

In our context, in what areas has the church become
worldly and in what ways are you temped to be worldly?
Five areas that we are uniquely tempted in our generation
come to mind. First is sexuality. Whether it is fornication,
homosexuality, or pornography, there are major temptations
to go the way of the world rather than the way of Christ. Related to this is gender. Scripture is clear that God has given
men and women different roles in marriage. Will we listen
to our feministic culture, or bow our knees to Scripture? We
are also tempted to "love the world" with our money. If sta-
tistics about giving are anywhere close to accurate, many
modern day Christians needs to repent of their greed and

---

[5] Arnold, *Three Crucial Questions about Spiritual Warfare*, 34.

[6] Kruse, *Letters of John*, 95.

begin seeking to live lives of generosity. Another temptation in contemporary culture is for the church to be "personality-driven" like the world. This is even a temptation in Reformed circles. We should honor men like John Piper, Mark Dever, R.C. Sproul, and Albert Mohler, but these men do not have a monopoly on the Holy Spirit. Beware the Reformed celebrity culture.

16 *For all that is in the world—the desires of the flesh and the desires of the eyes and pride in possessions—is not from the Father but is from the world.*

Now John defines *world* for us. John may be alluding to Eve in the garden of Eden here. The *desires of the flesh* is the tree that was good for food. The *desires of the eyes* could refer to the fruit that was a delight to the eyes. The *pride in possessions* could refer to the desire to possess God-like wisdom (Gen. 3:6).[7]

The *desires of the flesh* refers to sinful desires. The *desires of the eyes* refers to what we see. External things stimulate internal longing. For example, a person will be perfectly content with their shoes until they enter a shoe store and *see* all the new shoes. The *desire of the eyes* refers to greed, which we know from Colossians 3:5 and Ephesians 5:5 is the same as idolatry. *Pride in possessions*[8] refers to the way of life that thinks appearance and material possessions matter more than they really do.

---

[7] Kruse, *Letters of John,* 96 and Stott, *Letters of John,* 104, think the allusion is unlikely.

[8] Literally "pride of life" (*bios*), but the NT often uses this word to refer to property. See e.g., 1 John 3:17.

A good way to see if you are worldly is to look at your bank accounts and credit cards. Do you buy things for which you do not have the money? We have invented a civilized and more positive term for debt, namely credit.[9]

Greed is basically a problem of vision.[10] The urge to be rich will never go away in this age so we must redirect the desire to be rich in this life.[11] We should rather strive to be rich in the age to come, storing up treasures in heaven. What is the opposite of greed? Giving.[12] Seek to become a generous person. The best way to combat greed is by giving generously.

17 *And the world is passing away along with its desires, but whoever does the will of God abides forever.*

We saw above in 1 John 2:8 that the darkness is passing away, and the true light is already shining. Paul similarly said that *"the present form of this world is passing away"* (1 Cor. 7:31).

Doing the will of God is avoiding the world and all that is in it. Looking at the broader context of the letter, doing the will of God is believing in the Son and loving fellow Christians.[13]

Christians need long-term vision. We do not live for the moment. We must ask ourselves, "Do we really believe in eternity?" We shouldn't love the world because the new age is here, and the present evil age has its days numbered.

[9] Brian Rosner, *Beyond Greed*, (Australia: Matthias Media, 2004), 98.

[10] Ibid., 169.

[11] Ibid., 10, 170.

[12] Ibid., 121.

[13] Kruse, *Letters of John*, 97.

18 *Children, it is the last hour, and as you have heard that antichrist is coming, so now many antichrists have come. Therefore we know that it is the last hour.*

It is the last hour. We are in the final chapters of God's unfolding plan. The next great event in redemptive history will be its climax. John has already said that the darkness is passing away, and the true light is already shining (1 John 2.8), and the world is passing away (1 John 2:17). This is the same thing other New Testament writers mean by "last days." Acts 2:17 says, "*And in the last days it shall be, God declares, that I will pour out my Spirit on all flesh.*" These "last days" began at Pentecost. Hebrews 1:2 says, "*But in these last days he has spoken to us by his Son, whom he appointed the heir of all things, through whom also he created the world.*" For the author of Hebrews, these "last days" began with the incarnation. First Peter 1:20 says, "*He [Jesus] was foreknown before the foundation of the world but was made manifest in the last times for the sake of you.*" As with the author of Hebrews, Peter sees the last days being inaugurated with the coming of Christ.

John's first readers had been taught that antichrist would come, and John wants them to know that many antichrists have come. This is how we know it is the last hour. The word *antichrist* only occurs in John's letters. We learn from 1 John 2.22 that anyone who denies that Jesus is the Christ is the antichrist. From 1 John 4:3, we learn that every spirit that does not confess Jesus is the spirit of the antichrist. From 2 John 7, we learn that those who do not confess the coming of Jesus Christ in the flesh are antichrist.

When many Christians hear the word *antichrist*, they think of a very powerful end-time person. John teaches that there have already been antichrists, and more will come.

This does not necessarily preclude an end-time figure though. Second Thessalonians 2:3 speaks of a man of lawlessness who will come. Jesus spoke of false christs (Matt. 24:24, Mark 13:22). Revelation 12-13 speaks of the beast coming out of the sea. Taken all together, we get the picture of a great antichrist figure who will appear near the end as well as lesser antichrist figures throughout history.[14]

> 19 _They went out from us, but they were not of us; for if they had been of us, they would have continued with us. But they went out, that it might become plain that they all are not of us._

These antichrists were once part of the Christian community! How do you know if you are one of God's children? You remain faithful to the truth of God and the people of God. We all know people who at one point called themselves Christians but are no longer following the Lord. How are we to think of such people? Just last week I had lunch with a guy who made a profession of faith, was baptized, and seemed very zealous about the things of the Lord. At lunch, though, he informed me that "he was no longer a Christian." He said he did not regret the whole experience and learned from it, but he still had a lot of other ideas to research before he could call himself a Christian. Was this person ever a Christian? According to this verse, no. If he was truly one of us, he would have remained with us. We haven't seen him at our gatherings in weeks.

---

[14] Kruse, _Letters of John,_ 101; Marshall, _The Epistles of John,_ 151; Stott, _Letters of John,_ 108. For a good treatment of the antichrist from an amillennial perspective, see Kim Riddlebarger, _The Man of Sin_ (Grand Rapids: Baker Books, 2006).

One who is truly regenerate will remain in the truth and will remain with the people of God. Consider Romans chapter eight:

> And we know that for those who love God all things work together for good, for those who are called according to his purpose. For those whom he foreknew he also predestined to be conformed to the image of his Son, in order that he might be the firstborn among many brothers. And those whom he predestined he also called, and those whom he called he also justified, and those whom he justified he also glorified. What then shall we say to these things? If God is for us, who can be against us? He who did not spare his own Son but gave him up for us all, how will he not also with him graciously give us all things? Who shall bring any charge against God's elect? It is God who justifies. Who is to condemn? Christ Jesus is the one who died—more than that, who was raised—who is at the right hand of God, who indeed is interceding for us. Who shall separate us from the love of Christ? Shall tribulation, or distress, or persecution, or famine, or nakedness, or danger, or sword? As it is written, "For your sake we are being killed all the day long; we are regarded as sheep to be slaughtered." No, in all these things we are more than conquerors through him who loved us. For I am sure that neither death nor life, nor angels nor rulers, nor things present nor things to come, nor powers, nor height nor depth, nor anything else in all creation, will be able to separate us from the love of God in Christ Jesus our Lord. (Rom. 8:28-39)

God's love is effective. I have heard some say that we can still fall away of our own will, but in this passage, Paul lists everything that would cause a person to be tempted to turn from the Lord. In John 10:27-29, Jesus says, *"My sheep hear my voice, and I know them, and they follow me. I give them eternal life, and they will never perish, and no one will snatch them out of my hand. My Father, who has given them to me, is greater than all, and no one is able to snatch them out of the Father's hand."*

So the Baptist slogan, "once saved, always saved," is true, but it is not the whole story. The Calvinistic slogan "perseverance of the saints" is truer to Scripture. In Mark 13:13, Jesus says, _"The one who endures to the end will be saved,"_ not because salvation is the reward of endurance, but because endurance is the hallmark of the saved.[15] God's people _will_ persevere. Saving faith _always_ goes public in obedience and the transformation of lives.

>20-22 _But you have been anointed by the Holy One, and you all have knowledge. I write to you, not because you do not know the truth, but because you know it, and because no lie is of the truth. Who is the liar but he who denies that Jesus is the Christ? This is the antichrist, he who denies the Father and the Son._

John is confident that his hearers will persevere. He has the same mindset as the author of Hebrews, who after issuing severe warnings, says, _"Though we speak in this way, yet in your case, beloved, we feel sure of better things—things that belong to salvation"_ (Heb. 6:9).

Why will they persevere? Because they have the empowering presence of God. They have been anointed by the Holy One. I think John means that they have been anointed with the Holy Spirit _by_ Jesus the Holy One. The reason for this is that John refers to Jesus as the Holy One in John 6:69. Also, in John 14-16, Jesus says that _he_ will send the Spirit (see 15:26, 16:7, 16:12-15).[16]

Also, they all have knowledge. They don't need the additional teaching the false teachers were promoting. John has the promise of the new covenant in mind here. Jeremiah

---

[15] Stott, _Letters of John,_ 109.

[16] Kruse, _Letters of John,_ 103.

31:34 says, *"And no longer shall each one teach his neighbor and each his brother, saying, 'Know the LORD,' for they shall all know me, from the least of them to the greatest, declares the LORD"* (cf. John 6:45, 1 Thess. 4:9). As D.A. Carson notes, "Jeremiah does not so much anticipate the abolition of teachers as the abolition of mediating teachers, teachers with privileged access to God. Under the new covenant, there is no need for mediating teachers, for all know God, any more than for priests, for all are priests. Such teachers as the new covenant prescribes are seen as members of the body rather than as priestly mediators."[17]

John is simply recalling the truth they have already been taught. The false teachers are liars. They were denying that Jesus is the Christ. They are more than liars, they are antichrist! For John, the height of heresy is denying that Jesus was the Christ, the Son of God and Savior of the world.[18] They were claiming that Jesus was simply a mere man. In a word, they were denying the incarnation.[19] There are all sorts of ways that people do this today. Many cults can be dismissed based on this basic but fundamental test.

23 *No one who denies the Son has the Father. Whoever confesses the Son has the Father also.*

If you deny the Son, you deny the Father. Jesus is very clear about this in John's gospel:

_____

[17] D.A. Carson, "The Johannine Letters," in *New Dictionary of Biblical Theology,* ed. T. Desmond Alexander, Brian S. Rosner, D.A. Carson and Graeme Goldsworthy (Downers Grove, IL: IVP), 354.

[18] Marshall, *The Epistles of John,* 159.

[19] Stott, *Letters of John,* 115.

John 8:19—*They said to him therefore, "Where is your Father?" Jesus answered, "You know neither me nor my Father. If you knew me, you would know my Father also."*

John 8:42—*Jesus said to them, "If God were your Father, you would love me, for I came from God and I am here. I came not of my own accord, but he sent me."*

John 14:7—*If you had known me, you would have known my Father also. From now on you do know him and have seen him.*

John 14:21—*Whoever has my commandments and keeps them, he it is who loves me. And he who loves me will be loved by my Father, and I will love him and manifest myself to him.*

John 15:23—*Whoever hates me hates my Father also.*

This flies in the face of the common view of salvation. The common view is that all roads lead to the Father. In technical terms, this is known as universalism. In the end, all people will be saved according to universalists. More common among those who claim to follow Jesus is inclusivism. This view says that only Jesus saves, but not all people know that Jesus is saving them. Salvation is universally available to all, but is established by and leads to Christ. The Bible teaches exclusivism.[20] Only those who trust and follow Jesus will be saved. John says that anyone who denies the Son denies the Father. Jesus says that it is only through him that anyone can have access to the Father (John 14:6). Paul says there is only one mediator between God and humanity (1 Tim. 2:5). Peter said that salvation is found in no other name under heaven besides Jesus (Acts 4:12).

---

[20] See *Four Views on Salvation in a Pluralistic World*, ed. Stanley N. Gundry, Dennis L. Okholm, and Timothy R. Phillips (Grand Rapids: Zondervan, 1996).

24-25 Let what you heard from the beginning abide in you. If what you heard from the beginning abides in you, then you too will abide in the Son and in the Father. And this is the promise that he made to us—eternal life.

We must hold fast to the teaching of the apostles if we want to remain in communion with the Father and the Son. Doctrine matters, but it is important to keep in mind *which* doctrine John is referring to. It is not the minutia of so much doctrinal debate. It is clear from 1 John that what they have heard from the beginning is that Jesus is the Christ and his people are called to love their brothers and sisters as Christ has loved us.

How do we let what they heard from the beginning abide in us? We regularly read the Word on our own, in community, and we faithfully attend the worship gathering to hear the Word sung, read, and taught.

We must hold to this fundamental Christian teaching if we want to partake in the promise of eternal life. As mentioned above, eternal life is a certain quality of life here and now, but here John accents the future aspect of it. It has been *promised* to us who believe.

26-27 I write these things to you about those who are trying to deceive you. But the anointing that you received from him abides in you, and you have no need that anyone should teach you. But as his anointing teaches you about everything, and is true, and is no lie—just as it has taught you, abide in him.

John doesn't consider himself a teacher so much as one who reminds and exhorts his hearers to hold on to what they have already been taught. All in the new covenant have the Holy Spirit and have no need that anyone should teach them. This is very similar to what Paul says in 1 Thessalonians 4:9: "*Now concerning brotherly love you have no need for anyone to write to you, for you yourselves have been taught by God to love one another.*" Paul, like John, has the new covenant promises of Jeremiah 31 in the back of his mind as he writes.

We must abide in him who is true.

Chapter 6

1 John 2:28-3:10

And now, little children, abide in him, so that when he appears we may have confidence and not shrink from him in shame at his coming. If you know that he is righteous, you may be sure that everyone who practices righteousness has been born of him. See what kind of love the Father has given to us, that we should be called children of God; and so we are. The reason why the world does not know us is that it did not know him. Beloved, we are God's children now, and what we will be has not yet appeared; but we know that when he appears we shall be like him, because we shall see him as he is. And everyone who thus hopes in him purifies himself as he is pure. Everyone who makes a practice of sinning also practices lawlessness; sin is lawlessness. You know that he appeared to take away sins, and in him there is no sin. No one who abides in him keeps on sinning; no one who keeps on sinning has either seen him or known him. Little children, let no one deceive you. Whoever practices righteousness is righteous, as he is righteous. Whoever makes a practice of sinning is of the devil, for the devil has been sinning from the beginning. The reason the Son of God appeared was to destroy the works of the devil. No one born of God makes a practice of sinning, for God's seed abides in him, and he cannot keep on sinning because he has been born of God. By this it is evident who are the children of God, and who are the children of the devil: whoever does not practice righteousness is not of God, nor is the one who does not love his brother.

John now emphasizes the test of obedience.

28 *And now, little children, abide in him, so that when he appears we may have confidence and not shrink from him in shame at his coming.*

Abide in Jesus so that when he appears we may have confidence and not shame. Later, John will write, *"By this is love perfected with us, so that we may have confidence for the day of judgment, because as he is so also are we in this world"* (1 John 4:17). It is by abiding in Christ that we may have confidence for the day of judgment. To be confident here is defined as not shrinking in shame. Those who do not abide in the Son will shrink in shame because of their own unworthiness. Christ will put them to shame at his return. They will be openly disgraced at his coming.[1] As Charles Wesley sang in "And Can It Be," "bold I approach the eternal throne, and claim the crown through Christ my own."

29 *If you know that he is righteous, you may be sure that everyone who practices righteousness has been born of him.*

Part of what it means to abide in him is to practice righteousness. To practice righteousness is to do what is right. It refers to "correct moral behavior, acceptable to God."[2] We practice righteousness because we are born of him who is righteous. We are to strive to be like Jesus, the Righteous One.

This is the first of ten uses of the verb *to give birth to* (*gennaō*) in 1 John [see 2:29, 3:9 (2x), 4:7, 5:1 (3x), 5:4, 5:18 (2x)].[3] We now have a new relationship with God. He is our Father, and we are his children (cf. 1 John 3:1).

Notice John does not say that those who have been baptized may be sure that they have been born of God. Nor does he say those who have walked an aisle and prayed a prayer

---

[1] Marshall, *The Epistles of John*, 166.

[2] Ibid., 167.

[3] Kruse, *Letters of John*, 113-14.

may be sure that they have been born of God. No, John says
doing what is right is a sign that you are a child of God. We
must always look at the present as well as the past to gain
assurance.

> 3:1-3 *See what kind of love the Father has given to us, that we
> should be called children of God; and so we are. The reason why the
> world does not know us is that it did not know him. Beloved, we are
> God's children now, and what we will be has not yet appeared; but we
> know that when he appears we shall be like him, because we shall see
> him as he is. And everyone who thus hopes in him purifies himself as
> he is pure.*

All too often we do not appreciate the amazing reality
that we are children of God. We are! The Father has said so.
This is our assurance here and now.[4] In the midst of difficult
jobs, health problems, money problems, difficult children,
difficult parents, and all the problems and challenges we
face, it is good to be reminded that we are children of the
living God. The love of God is a gift of God.

The world doesn't "get" us because it does not know Jesus or the world-changing implications of his coming. This
is also further proof that we are children of God. We should
rub some people the wrong way. In 1 John 3:13, he says, *"Do
not be surprised, brothers, that the world hates you."*

What we will be has not yet appeared. We are not sure
what our resurrection bodies will be like. As Paul puts it in 1
Corinthians 2:9, *"But, as it is written, 'What no eye has seen, nor
ear heard, nor the heart of man imagined, what God has prepared
for those who love him.'"*

---

[4] For an excellent treatment of this reality, see Sinclair Ferguson's *Children of the Living God.*

But we do know that when he appears, we will become fully like him. All of life for the believer is about conformity to Christ. That is our aim in this life, and it will not be fully consummated until the Lord returns. Romans 8:29-30 says, *"For those whom he foreknew he also predestined to be conformed to the image of his Son, in order that he might be the firstborn among many brothers. And those whom he predestined he also called, and those whom he called he also justified, and those whom he justified he also glorified."* This is a glorious passage. God's grand purpose is that we be conformed to the image of Christ. This process will continue until the Lord returns. Then, we will be fully conformed to Jesus. As Paul says elsewhere, *"But our citizenship is in heaven, and from it we await a Savior, the Lord Jesus Christ, who will transform our low- ly body to be like his glorious body, by the power that enables him even to subject all things to himself"* (Phil. 3:20-21). John says that when he appears we will be like him because we will see him as he is. This process starts now though: *"And we all, with unveiled face, beholding the glory of the Lord, are being transformed into the same image from one degree of glory to an- other"* (2 Cor. 3:18). We become like Jesus as we behold Jesus.

From the verses that follow, we see that purity for John means freedom from sin.[5] How does this hope purify? It puts things into perspective. It causes us to begin now to live the life we will live forever.

> 4-5 *Everyone who makes a practice of sinning also practices law-* *lessness; sin is lawlessness. You know that he appeared to take away* *sins, and in him there is no sin.*

---

5 Marshall, *The Epistles of John*, 174.

Sin is lawlessness. The false teachers were teaching that believers did not have to take sin very seriously (1 John 1:8-9), but John disagrees. Sin is active rebellion against God's will.

It is interesting that John defines sin as lawlessness (*anomia*). This is the only time the word *lawlessness* is used in the letter, and the word *law* does not appear at all. It could be that John means that sin is breaking God's law, but that would leave his readers wondering which law they have broken.[6] As Kruse puts it, "It does not here carry the idea of breaking the law, for the whole question of the law is absent from this letter."[7] It is more probable, as I. Howard Marshall and Colin Kruse argue, that John is using the word lawlessness in the same way Paul used it in 2 Thessalonians where he speaks of the man of lawlessness (2 Thess. 2:3) and the mystery of lawlessness (2 Thess. 2:7). There the word is associated with the final outbreak of evil against Christ and signifies rebellion against the will of God. So for John, to commit sin is to place oneself on the side of the devil and the antichrist and to stand in opposition to Jesus.[8]

Jesus appeared to take away sins. In his gospel, John recorded John the Baptist saying, *"Behold, the Lamb of God, who takes away the sin of the world!"* John has already said that Jesus is the propitiation for our sins (1 John 2:2) and that the

[6] Some insist that John is referring to the Decalogue, but this is impossible since the witness of the NT is univocal in insisting that new covenant believers are no longer under the law. The old covenant ceased with the coming of Christ and has been replaced by the new and better covenant in Christ and his Spirit.

[7] Kruse, *Letters of John*, 117.

[8] Marshall, *The Epistles of John*, 176; Kruse, *Letters of John*, 117-19.

blood of Jesus cleanses us from all sin (1 John 1:7). We noted that behind this word lays the notion of expiation *and* propitiation. In this verse, John is accenting the expiatory nature of the cross. It takes away sin. It takes away both the penalty and the power of sin.

In Jesus there is no sin; he is the righteous one (1 John 2:1); he is the pure one (1 John 3:3).[9] This is how he alone, is able to take away our sin. The New Testament teaches the sinlessness of Jesus many times:

2 Cor. 5:21—*For our sake he made him to be sin who knew no sin, so that in him we might become the righteousness of God.*

Heb. 4:15—*For we do not have a high priest who is unable to sympathize with our weaknesses, but one who in every respect has been tempted as we are, yet without sin.*

1 Pet. 2:22—*He committed no sin, neither was deceit found in his mouth.* The point is that Jesus stands in opposition to sin and his people must do the same.[10]

6-7 *No one who abides in him keeps on sinning; no one who keeps on sinning has either seen him or known him. Little children, let no one deceive you. Whoever practices righteousness is righteous, as he is righteous.*

What are we to do with these verses? This is a striking statement from John. He has already stated that the person who says he has no sin is a liar and the truth is not in him (1 John 1:8-10). John is referring to habitual sin here. This is the view of the ESV and NIV, which translates the literal "everyone who abides in him does not sin" as "no one who abides in him keeps on sinning" to signify the continual na-

---

[9] Kruse, *Letters of John*, 119.

[10] Marshall, *The Epistles of John*, 177.

ture of the sin. John is not speaking of perfection but of the pattern and direction of a person's life.[11] Christians fall into sin; they do not dive into it or walk in it.

John does not want his hearers to be deceived. It is not about what a person *says*, but what a person *practices*. The false teachers "talked the talk" but did not "walk the walk."

> 8-10 *If we say we have no sin, we deceive ourselves, and the truth is not in us. If we confess our sins, he is faithful and just to forgive us our sins and to cleanse us from all unrighteousness. If we say we have not sinned, we make him a liar, and his word is not in us.*

People who have the devil for their father act like the devil (John 8:44), who has been sinning from the beginning. John is surely alluding to the first chapters of the Bible with this comment. People who fail to do righteousness do not belong to God, but to God's enemy.[12] Since Jesus came to take away sin and destroy the works of the devil, it should be clear that Christians cannot compromise with either.[13]

The New Testament presents the cross of Christ as a multi-faceted diamond. The writers of Scripture use many metaphors to describe the work of Christ. Because of this, theologians have come up with various "theories" to describe the atonement. On the cross, Jesus gives us a moral example (moral influence theory), holds up the justice of God (governmental theory), paid the penalty for our sins (penal substitution), and defeats Satan and his demons (*Christus Victor* theory). Many traditions major on only one theme, but as

---

[11] Thomas R. Schreiner, *New Testament Theology* (Grand Rapids: Baker, 2008), 568; Stott, *Letters of John,* 129, 137-38.

[12] Marshall, *The Epistles of John,* 185.

[13] Stott, *Letters of John,* 128.

Scot McKnight points out, the Bible gives us "a whole bag of clubs," and it would be foolish to play golf with only one club when others are readily available.[14]

Here in 1 John 3:8, we have a key verse supporting the *Christus Victor* theme, which is about the victory of Jesus Christ over all the powers of evil and darkness.[15]

Greg Boyd writes, "The first messianic prophecy given in Scripture—indeed the first prophecy period—announced just this: a descendent of Eve would crush the head of the serpent who originally deceived humanity into joining in his rebellion (Gen. 3:15). It is therefore not surprising that the original disciples expressed what the Messiah accomplished in terms of *a victory over the ancient serpent.*"[16] Christus Victor is a major New Testament theme:

> John 12:31—*Now is the judgment of this world; now will the ruler of this world be cast out.*

> Heb. 2:14—*Since therefore the children share in flesh and blood, he himself likewise partook of the same things, that through death he might destroy the one who has the power of death, that is, the devil.*

> Eph. 1:20-21—*That he worked in Christ when he raised him from the dead and seated him at his right hand in the heavenly places, far above all rule and authority and power and dominion, and above every name that is named, not only in this age but also in the one to come.*

---

[14] Scot McKnight, *A Community Called Atonement* (Nashville: Abingdon, 2007), xiii.

[15] N.T. Wright, *Evil and the Justice of God* (Downers Grove, IL: IVP, 2006), 95, 114.

[16] Gregory A. Boyd, "Christus Victor View," in *The Nature of the Atonement,* ed. James Beilby and Paul R. Eddy (Downers Grove, IL: IVP Academic, 2006), 30.

Eph. 3:10—*So that through the church the manifold wisdom of God might now be made known to the rulers and authorities in the heavenly places.*

Col. 2:13-15—*And you, who were dead in your trespasses and the uncircumcision of your flesh, God made alive together with him, having forgiven us all our trespasses, by canceling the record of debt that stood against us with its legal demands. This he set aside, nailing it to the cross. He disarmed the rulers and authorities and put them to open shame, by triumphing over them in him.*

1 Cor. 15:25—*For he must reign until he has put all his enemies under his feet.*

Rev. 20:3—*And threw him into the pit, and shut it and sealed it over him, so that he might not deceive the nations any longer.*

True Christians do not make a practice of sinning. We do still stumble in many ways (James 3:2), but we must take a step back and look at the trajectory of our lives. Are we growing in Christ? If not, we need to ask some hard questions. If we make a practice of sin, we are not truly saved.

Christians do not make a practice of sinning because God's seed abides in him. John uses the metaphor of a seed planted in the heart which produces new life.[17] Being born of God is a deep, radical, inward transformation.[18]

John also says we must love one another. If we do not love our brothers and sisters in Christ, we are children of the devil. John will develop this theme further in the next section.

---

[17] Marshall, *The Epistles of John*, 186.

[18] Stott, *Letters of John*, 130.

Chapter 7

1 John 3:11-24

For this is the message that you have heard from the beginning, that we should love one another. We should not be like Cain, who was of the evil one and murdered his brother. And why did he murder him? Because his own deeds were evil and his brother's righteous. Do not be surprised, brothers, that the world hates you. We know that we have passed out of death into life, because we love the brothers. Whoever does not love abides in death. Everyone who hates his brother is a murderer, and you know that no murderer has eternal life abiding in him. By this we know love, that he laid down his life for us, and we ought to lay down our lives for the brothers. But if anyone has the world's goods and sees his brother in need, yet closes his heart against him, how does God's love abide in him? Little children, let us not love in word or talk but in deed and in truth. By this we shall know that we are of the truth and reassure our heart before him; for whenever our heart condemns us, God is greater than our heart, and he knows everything. Beloved, if our heart does not condemn us, we have confidence before God; and whatever we ask we receive from him, because we keep his commandments and do what pleases him. And this is his commandment, that we believe in the name of his Son Jesus Christ and love one another, just as he has commanded us. Whoever keeps his commandments abides in God, and God in him. And by this we know that he abides in us, by the Spirit whom he has given us.

Now, John will focus on the test of love.

11-12 *For this is the message that you have heard from the beginning, that we should love one another. We should not be like Cain, who was of the evil one and murdered his brother. And why did he murder him? Because his own deeds were evil and his brother's righteous.*

John is constantly reminding his readers what they have heard from the beginning (of their Christian experience). He does this at various points in this short letter:

> 1 John 2:7—*Beloved, I am writing you no new commandment, but an old commandment that you had from the beginning. The old commandment is the word that you have heard.*

> 1 John 2:24—*Let what you heard from the beginning abide in you. If what you heard from the beginning abides in you, then you too will abide in the Son and in the Father.*

> 2 John 1:5-6—*And now I ask you, dear lady—not as though I were writing you a new commandment, but the one we have had from the beginning—that we love one another. And this is love, that we walk according to his commandments; this is the commandment, just as you have heard from the beginning, so that you should walk in it.*

The message they have heard is that they should love one another. This is so central for the apostle John. This was the central message taken from Jesus: "*A new commandment I give to you, that you love one another: just as I have loved you, you also are to love one another. By this all people will know that you are my disciples, if you have love for one another*" (John 13:34-35). Cain was the complete opposite of loving (Gen. 4:1-25, Heb. 11:4). He was evil like his father (John 8:46).

> 13 *Do not be surprised, brothers, that the world hates you.*

Cain was a prototype of the world.[1] In a verse that almost seems like a parenthetical comment, John reminds his readers that they must love even while being hated by the world.[2] As mentioned at 1 John 2:2, *world* is used 23 times by John, and its meaning varies with context. Here he simply

---

[1] Stott, *Letters of John*, 142.

[2] Marshall, *The Epistles of John*, 190.

means the unbelieving world, which now includes the false teachers in John's mind (1 John 2:18-19).[3] Why would the world hate us? Several reasons could be given. They may hate our message. This is particularly true for the exclusive nature of the gospel. Or it could be our belief in hell, which is related to exclusivism. It may be our moral judgments. It could be that Christianity calls their autonomy into question. They may hate us because we bring out their guilt. Or it could simply be that they are acting in accord with their ultimate leader, Satan.

Does the world hate you? This is a question we must ask. We should strive to be at peace with all people, but occasionally we should feel hated. If not, we must examine our lives and ask if we are living in a distinctively Christian manner.

> 14-15 *We know that we have passed out of death into life, because we love the brothers. Whoever does not love abides in death. Everyone who hates his brother is a murderer, and you know that no murderer has eternal life abiding in him.*

The world hates, but we love one another. As John shows us again and again, part of the core of Jesus' word is that we love one another. This is a surprising statement from John. How do we know if we have this resurrection life according to John? The way we know we have passed from death to life is if we love one another. It is important to point out that mutual love is the evidence, not basis, for new life. Still, John teaches that assurance is dependent upon our love for fellow believers. In his gospel, John wrote, *"Truly, truly, I say to you, whoever hears my word and believes him who sent me has eternal*

---

[3] Kruse, *Letters of John*, 134-35.

life. He does not come into judgment, but has passed from death to life" (John 5:24). Through belief in Jesus and loving one another, we already have resurrection life. As Paul writes in Ephesians 2:4-5, *"But God, being rich in mercy, because of the great love with which he loved us, even when we were dead in our trespasses, made us alive together with Christ."*

On the other hand, everyone who hates his brother or sister is a murderer. Jesus had something similar to say in Matthew 5:21-24: *"You have heard that it was said to those of old, 'You shall not murder; and whoever murders will be liable to judgment.' But I say to you that everyone who is angry with his brother will be liable to judgment; whoever insults his brother will be liable to the council; and whoever says, 'You fool!' will be liable to the hell of fire. So if you are offering your gift at the altar and there remember that your brother has something against you, leave your gift there before the altar and go. First be reconciled to your brother, and then come and offer your gift."* Hatred is incompatible with the Christian life. It is tantamount to murder, for when you hate someone, you wish them gone.[4] As Calvin put it, "for we wish him to perish whom we hate."[5]

Americans, with our cherished autonomy and individualism, need to hear and heed these words. Vertical love must demonstrate itself in horizontal love. John is clear about this. In 1 John 4:12, he said, *"No one has ever seen God; if we love one another, God abides in us and his love is perfected in us."* In 1 John 4:20, he said, *"If anyone says, 'I love God,' and hates his brother, he is a liar; for he who does not love his brother whom he has seen cannot love God whom he has not seen."* Love for God

---

[4] Marshall, *Epistles of John*, 191-92.

[5] Quoted in Stott, *Letters of John*, 144.

necessarily issues in love for fellow Christians. Listen to the stunning words of Luke 10:25-28: *"And behold, a lawyer stood up to put him to the test, saying, 'Teacher, what shall I do to inherit eternal life?' He said to him, 'What is written in the Law? How do you read it?' And he answered, 'You shall love the Lord your God with all your heart and with all your soul and with all your strength and with all your mind, and your neighbor as yourself.' And he said to him, 'You have answered correctly; do this, and you will live.'"*

As Stott writes, "Great stress is laid in the New Testament on love as the pre-eminent Christian virtue, the firstfruit of the Spirit (Gal. 5:22), the sign of the reality of faith (Gal. 5:6), and the greatest of the three abiding Christian graces, which never ends and without which we are 'nothing' (1 Cor. 13:2, 8, 13)."[6]

> 16 *By this we know love, that he laid down his life for us, and we ought to lay down our lives for the brothers.*

Love is such a plastic word in our culture. I love my son Josiah, and I love Chinese food. Hopefully, these are two different types of love. As N.T. Wright says, "The English word 'love' is trying to do so many different jobs at the same time that someone really ought to sit down with it and teach it how to delegate."[7] Love is not simply an emotion, but self-giving action for the benefit of others.[8] Love is humble ser-

---

[6] Stott, *Letters of John*, 143.

[7] N.T. Wright, *After You Believe: Why Christian Character Matters* (New York: HarperOne, 2010), 183.

[8] D.S. Dockery, "Fruit of the Spirit," in *Dictionary of Paul and His Letters* (Downers Grove, IL: IVP, 1993), 318. Fee says it is "self-sacrificially giving oneself for others," *God's Empowering Presence*, 447. Gorman says "Love is characterized by self-giving for the good of others,"

vice of others.[9] Love expends itself in the interests of others,[10] as the essence of love is self-sacrifice.[11]

Tom Schreiner defines love as "giving oneself for others, so that they are encouraged and strengthened to give themselves more fully to God."[12] Love is helping a person glorify God. With Jesus' act of love in mind, Paul Tripp defines love as "willing self-sacrifice for the good of another that does not require reciprocation or that the person being loved is deserving of."[13]

Jesus is the paradigm for love.[14] He laid down his life for us. He is the pattern of love. As he laid down his life, we are to lay down our lives. His love is status-renouncing, self-giving, and others-oriented.[15] John has already held out Jesus as an example several times in his letter:

Cruciformity, 160. Marshall says, "Love means readiness to do anything for other people," Marshall, *Epistles of John*, 192.

[9] Hays, *Moral Vision*, 144.

[10] Kruse, *Letters of John*, 137.

[11] Stott, *Letters of John*, 144.

[12] Schreiner, *Galatians*, 319.

[13] Paul David Tripp, *What Did You Expect?* (Wheaton, IL: Crossway, 2010), 188.

[14] Sadly, this is a neglected theme. Richard Hays does a fine job emphasizing this *emphasized* biblical theme in his *Moral Vision of the NT*. See pages 27, 29, 31, 46, 120ff, 144-45, 197. Also see Michael Gorman's *Cruciformity* and Luke Timothy Johnson's *Living Jesus* (New York: HarperOne, 1999). Don't miss Jason B. Hood's important article "The Cross in the New Testament: Two Theses in Conversation with Recent Literature," *WTJ* 71 2009.

[15] Gorman, *Cruciformity*, 174.

1 John 1:7—*But if we walk in the light, as he is in the light, we have fellowship with one another, and the blood of Jesus his Son cleanses us from all sin.*

1 John 2:6—*Whoever says he abides in him ought to walk in the same way in which he walked.*

1 John 3:3—*And everyone who thus hopes in him purifies himself as he is pure.*

1 John 3:7—*Little children, let no one deceive you. Whoever practices righteousness is righteous, as he is righteous.*

1 John 4:11—*Beloved, if God so loved us, we also ought to love one another.*

This is a theme found all throughout the New Testament. Consider just four clear and important passages:

John 15:12—*This is my commandment, that you love one another as I have loved you.*

Phil. 2:3-8—*Do nothing from rivalry or conceit, but in humility count others more significant than yourselves. Let each of you look not only to his own interests, but also to the interests of others. Have this mind among yourselves, which is yours in Christ Jesus, who, though he was in the form of God, did not count equality with God a thing to be grasped, but made himself nothing, taking the form of a servant, being born in the likeness of men. And being found in human form, he humbled himself by becoming obedient to the point of death, even death on a cross.*

1 Pet. 2:21—*For to this you have been called, because Christ also suffered for you, leaving you an example, so that you might follow in his steps.*

Rom. 15:1-3—*We who are strong have an obligation to bear with the failings of the weak, and not to please ourselves. Let each of us please his neighbor for his good, to build him up. For Christ did not please himself, but as it is written, "The reproaches of those who reproached you fell on me."* (cf. 1 Cor. 11:1, 2 Cor. 8:9, 10:1)

Christus exemplar or *imitatio Christi* is a central theme in the New Testament. Reformed Christians have neglected this theme, too often associating it with liberals who deny penal substitution. But Christians are called to walk in love as Christ loved us; we are to seek to please our neighbor because Christ did not please himself; we are to forgive one another even as Christ forgave us; we are to be conformed to the image of his Son, till we all come to the measure of the stature of the fullness of Christ; we are to lay down our lives for our fellow Christians as Christ laid down his life for us; we are to love him because he first loved us; we are to walk in the light as he is in the light; we are called to walk as Jesus walked; we are called to suffer like Christ who left us an example to follow in his steps; we are to run looking to Jesus; we are summoned to go outside the camp because Jesus suffered outside the gate.[16]

Jesus looked away from his own self-interests and to the interest of others. To imitate Jesus is to follow his example of surrendering our own prerogatives and interests.[17] As Wolfgang Schrage put it, "Conformity to Christ and to his love determines the entire way Christians live."[18] His life is the guiding principle for our lives.

17-18 *But if anyone has the world's goods and sees his brother in need, yet closes his heart against him, how does God's love abide in him? Little children, let us not love in word or talk but in deed and in truth.*

---

[16] White, *Biblical Ethics,* 110.

[17] Hays, *Moral Vision,* 46.

[18] Schrage, *The Ethics of the NT,* 308.

John doesn't leave us in the abstract about love. It's easy to *say* we will lay our lives down for our brothers and sisters because the reality of that happening is rare.

The switch from the plural *brothers* in verse 16 to the singular *brother* in verse 17 is deliberate. It is easy to say we love "the church," without having to give of self in specific ways for specific individuals. Loving everyone may be an excuse for loving no one.[19] Love must be prepared to meet the needs of others whatever the cost in self-sacrifice."[20] *Goods* in verse 17 is the same word for possessions in 1 John 2:17 (*bios*).

The background of John's thinking here may be Deuteronomy 15:7-9, which reads, *"If among you, one of your brothers should become poor, in any of your towns within your land that the LORD your God is giving you, you shall not harden your heart or shut your hand against your poor brother, but you shall open your hand to him and lend him sufficient for his need, whatever it may be. Take care lest there be an unworthy thought in your heart and you say, 'The seventh year, the year of release is near,' and your eye look grudgingly on your poor brother, and you give him nothing, and he cry to the LORD against you, and you be guilty of sin."*[21]

When John says that God's love does not abide in the one who lacks pity for his brothers and sisters, is he referring to God's love for us or our love for God? It is difficult to tell, and John may mean both. For the New Testament, our love for God is always a result and response to his love for us. I

---

[19] Stott, *Letters of John*, 145.

[20] Marshall, *Epistles of John*, 194.

[21] Kruse, *Letters of John*, 138.

tend to think that John means our love for God, though, because in 1 John 4:20, he says, *"If anyone says, 'I love God,' and
hates his brother, he is a liar; for he who does not love his brother
whom he has seen cannot love God whom he has not seen."*[22] This
is very similar to James' concern, when he writes, *"If a brother or sister is poorly clothed and lacking in daily food, and one of
you says to them, 'Go in peace, be warmed and filled,' without giving them the things needed for the body, what good is that?"*
(James 2:15-16). I. Howard Marshall writes, "The tragedy is
that we have not learned to take this seriously. The need of
the world is not for heroic acts of martyrdom, but for heroic
acts of material sacrifice. If I am a well-off Christian, while
others are poor, I am not acting as a true Christian."[23] Ouch
and amen!

> 19-22 *By this we shall know that we are of the truth and reassure
> our heart before him; for whenever our heart condemns us, God is
> greater than our heart, and he knows everything. Beloved, if our heart
> does not condemn us, we have confidence before God; and whatever
> we ask we receive from him, because we keep his commandments and
> do what pleases him.*

The word here for *reassure* is *peithō*, which occurs 52 times
in the New Testament *and* never means "reassure!" It usual-
ly means "convince."[24] Rather than act naturally by avoiding
those in need, we must *persuade* our hearts. This persuasion
must take place whenever our hearts condemn us, that is,
when we are tempted to avoid selfless generosity towards
those in need. God is greater than our hearts, that is, he is

---

[22] *Contra* Stott, *Letters of John*, 145.

[23] Marshall, *Epistles of John*, 196.

[24] Kruse, *Letters of John*, 140. I am indebted to Kruse's exegesis for the following paragraph.

not tempted to be greedy like we are. His generosity, self-lessness, and compassion towards the needy are much greater than ours. This should function as a reason for us to overcome our own selfishness and seek to be like our God (godly). He knows everything. Kruse writes, "In summary, verses 19-20 function as a stern warning against that mean-ness of heart which objects to our expending material re-sources to meet the needs of fellow believers, and provide a foil for the positive reinforcement of generosity offered in verses 21-22."[25]

We will know we are of the truth when our love finds ex-pression in helping our needy brothers and sisters.[26] We have confidence before God when we are keeping his com-mands and pleasing him.

Obedience is the condition, not the cause, of answered prayer.[27] In 1 John 5:14, John adds that he hears us whenever we ask in accordance with his will (cf. John 14:14, 16:23).

> 23 *And this is his commandment, that we believe in the name of his Son Jesus Christ and love one another, just as he has commanded us.*

Belief in the Son is God's fundamental command to hu-man beings.

Belief and love go together, and neither is sufficient with-out the other.[28] Not surprisingly, this is the same outlook as the apostle Paul. For him, the only thing that has value is *faith working through love* (Gal. 5:6).

---

25 Ibid., 141.

26 Ibid., 141.

27 Stott, *Letters of John*, 150.

28 Marshall, *Epistles of John*, 201; Stott, *Letters of John*, 151.

24 *Whoever keeps his commandments abides in him, and he in them. And by this we know that he abides in us, by the Spirit whom he has given us.*

Here we have a nice summary statement for this section. Living in God is our new spiritual existence characterized by joyful obedience. John taught the same idea in the fifteenth chapter of his gospel:

Abide in me, and I in you. As the branch cannot bear fruit by itself, unless it abides in the vine, neither can you, unless you abide in me. I am the vine; you are the branches. Whoever abides in me and I in him, he it is that bears much fruit, for apart from me you can do nothing. If anyone does not abide in me he is thrown away like a branch and withers; and the branches are gathered, thrown into the fire, and burned. If you abide in me, and my words abide in you, ask whatever you wish, and it will be done for you. By this my Father is glorified, that you bear much fruit and so prove to be my disciples. As the Father has loved me, so have I loved you. Abide in my love. If you keep my commandments, you will abide in my love, just as I have kept my Father's commandments and abide in his love. These things I have spoken to you, that my joy may be in you, and that your joy may be full (John 15:4-11).

This is the first of several references to the Spirit in 1 John:

1 John 4:2—*By this you know the Spirit of God: every spirit that confesses that Jesus Christ has come in the flesh is from God.*

1 John 4:6—*We are from God. Whoever knows God listens to us; whoever is not from God does not listen to us. By this we know the Spirit of truth and the spirit of error.*

1 John 4:13—*By this we know that we abide in him and he in us, because he has given us of his Spirit.*

1 John 5:6—*This is he who came by water and blood—Jesus Christ; not by the water only but by the water and the blood. And the Spirit is the one who testifies, because the Spirit is the truth.*

The presence of the Spirit gives us assurance. In Romans 8:14-16, Paul writes, *"For all who are led by the Spirit of God are sons of God. For you did not receive the spirit of slavery to fall back into fear, but you have received the Spirit of adoption as sons, by whom we cry, 'Abba! Father!' The Spirit himself bears witness with our spirit that we are children of God."* If we have the Spirit, we will confess Jesus as the Christ and will love our brothers and sisters (Gal. 5:13-26).

Chapter 8

1 John 4:1-12

Beloved, do not believe every spirit, but test the spirits to see whether they are from God, for many false prophets have gone out into the world. By this you know the Spirit of God: every spirit that confesses that Jesus Christ has come in the flesh is from God, and every spirit that does not confess Jesus is not from God. This is the spirit of the antichrist, which you heard was coming and now is in the world already. Little children, you are from God and have overcome them, for he who is in you is greater than he who is in the world. They are from the world; therefore they speak from the world, and the world listens to them. We are from God. Whoever knows God listens to us; whoever is not from God does not listen to us. By this we know the Spirit of truth and the spirit of error. Beloved, let us love one another, for love is from God, and whoever loves has been born of God and knows God. Anyone who does not love does not know God, because God is love. In this the love of God was made manifest among us, that God sent his only Son into the world, so that we might live through him. In this is love, not that we have loved God but that he loved us and sent his Son to be the propitiation for our sins. Beloved, if God so loved us, we also ought to love one another. No one has ever seen God; if we love one another, God abides in us and his love is perfected in us.

1-3 *Beloved, do not believe every spirit, but test the spirits to see whether they are from God, for many false prophets have gone out into the world. By this you know the Spirit of God: every spirit that confesses that Jesus Christ has come in the flesh is from God, and every spirit that does not confess Jesus is not from God. This is the spirit of the antichrist, which you heard was coming and now is in the world already.*

Now John returns to the test of true belief. John tells us we need to test the spirits because not every spirit is from God. This is similar to what Paul said in 1 Thessalonians 5:19-22: *"Do not quench the Spirit. Do not despise prophecies, but test everything; hold fast what is good. Abstain from every form of evil."* John also tells us how to test the spirits. The word *spirit* here probably means an utterance inspired by a spirit or a person inspired by a spirit.[1] He says we can recognize the Spirit of God by whether or not it confesses that Jesus Christ has come in the flesh. Comparing this passage with 1 John 2:23, we see that those who deny the Son have neither the Father nor the Spirit.[2]

This is John's test of doctrinal orthodoxy. Any spirit that does not believe that Jesus has come in the flesh from God is the spirit of the antichrist, which is coming and is already in the world. First Corinthians 12:3 says, *"Therefore I want you to understand that no one speaking in the Spirit of God ever says 'Jesus is accursed!' and no one can say 'Jesus is Lord' except in the Holy Spirit."*

Even evil spirits recognized the deity of Jesus during his earthly ministry (Mark 1:24, 3:11; 4:7-8) but did not acknowledge him as Lord. The Spirit of God, on the other hand, always honors the Son.[3] Consider John's teaching in his gospel:

> John 15:26—*But when the Helper comes, whom I will send to you from the Father, the Spirit of truth, who proceeds from the Father, he will bear witness about me.*

---

[1] Marshall, *Epistles of John*, 204.

[2] Stott, *Letters of John*, 156.

[3] Ibid., 155.

John 16:13-15—*When the Spirit of truth comes, he will guide you into all the truth, for he will not speak on his own authority, but whatever he hears he will speak, and he will declare to you the things that are to come. He will glorify me, for he will take what is mine and declare it to you. All that the Father has is mine; therefore I said that he will take what is mine and declare it to you.*

The spirit of the antichrist has been active since the first century and has continually tried to influence people away from true Christianity (1 John 2:18, 22). Second John 1:7 says, *"For many deceivers have gone out into the world, those who do not confess the coming of Jesus Christ in the flesh. Such a one is the deceiver and the antichrist."*

False teachers were saying that Jesus only appeared to be human, denying his humanity. This was because in their view, material creation was evil, which would, of course, include physical bodies. The New Testament speaks of the reality of false prophets in several places:[4]

Matt. 7:15—*Beware of false prophets, who come to you in sheep's clothing but inwardly are ravenous wolves.*

Matt. 24:11—*And many false prophets will arise and lead many astray.*

2 Pet. 2:1—*But false prophets also arose among the people, just as there will be false teachers among you, who will secretly bring in destructive heresies, even denying the Master who bought them, bringing upon themselves swift destruction.*

This false teaching is prevalent in our day. Jesus is "cool" today. Many believe that Jesus lived a good life and taught many wonderful things. Most religions affirm this. John says we must affirm both the full deity and humanity of Jesus, or

---

[4] Kruse, *Letters of John*, 145.

we are not truly "confessing Jesus." As John Stott puts it, "The fundamental Christian doctrine which can never be compromised concerns the eternal divine-human person of Jesus Christ, the Son of God."[5] Those who deny this elementary truth are of the spirit of antichrist.

> 4-5 *Little children, you are from God and have overcome them, for he who is in you is greater than he who is in the world. They are from the world; therefore they speak from the world, and the world listens to them.*

John reassures his readers that they are of God. They are born of God and are children of God. His readers have overcome the false teachers, not meaning a physical beating, but they have proved victorious over the temptation to follow the false teaching.[6] They have overcome by rejecting the false teaching and the false teachers. We overcome because we are on God's team. We overcome because God overcomes. As Jesus said in John 16:33, *"I have said these things to you, that in me you may have peace. In the world you will have tribulation. But take heart; I have overcome the world."*

He who is in the world suggests an identification with the *ruler of this world* in John's gospel, which is Satan, and by extension, his demons:[7]

> John 12:31—*Now is the judgment of this world; now will the ruler of this world be cast out.*

> John 14:30—*I will no longer talk much with you, for the ruler of this world is coming. He has no claim on me.*

---

[5] Stott, *Letters of John*, 155.

[6] Marshall, *Epistles of John*, 208.

[7] Kruse, *Letters of John*, 149.

John 16:11—*Concerning judgment, because the ruler of this world is judged.*

World here means humanity in opposition to its maker and the evil attitude characteristic of this people.[8] The false teachers are now part of the world and speak from the viewpoint of this world, having left the community of believers. They now lay in the power of the evil one (1 John 5:19). It is satanic to deny the incarnation.

6 *We are from God. Whoever knows God listens to us; whoever is not from God does not listen to us. By this we know the Spirit of truth and the spirit of error.*

Here we have a second way to test the spirits. Do they confess Jesus Christ the Son of God come in the flesh, and are they responsive to the message of the apostles? Whoever knows God listens to the apostles. What does that mean for us? It means that those who know God listen to the New Testament. A person who will not listen to the apostles shows that he is the spirit of falsehood rather than of truth.

7-8 *Beloved, let us love one another, for love is from God, and whoever loves has been born of God and knows God. Anyone who does not love does not know God, because God is love.*

As William Tyndale put it, "John singeth his old song again."[9] Love comes from God; therefore, those who love come from him as well. Of course, we know from the rest of the letter that love is not the only criterion for the children of God (cf. 1 John 3:23). John has three great expressions on the

---

[8] Marshall, *Epistles of John*, 209.

[9] Quoted in Stott, *Letters of John*, 160.

nature of God: God is light (1:5), God is love (4:8), and God is spirit (4:24).[10]

God is love. He is the great giver. He continually gives of himself for the good of his people. Love is not God's only attribute, but it is his essential essence. We saw this from Exodus 34:6-7: *"The LORD passed before him and proclaimed, 'The LORD, the LORD, a God merciful and gracious, slow to anger, and abounding in steadfast love and faithfulness, keeping steadfast love for thousands, forgiving iniquity and transgression and sin, but who will by no means clear the guilty, visiting the iniquity of the fathers on the children and the children's children, to the third and the fourth generation.'"*

9-10 *In this the love of God was made manifest among us, that God sent his only Son into the world, so that we might live through him. In this is love, not that we have loved God but that he loved us and sent his Son to be the propitiation for our sins.*

The fact that God sent his Son shows that the Son was preexistent. God sent his *only Son*. The NIV is better here with *one and only (monogenēs)*. The idea is that Jesus is unique. Jesus is God's *only* Son (cf. Heb. 11:17, Luke 7:12, John 1:14, 18, 3:16, 18).

At 1 John 2:2, we showed that the word *propitiation* contains both the notion of removing God's wrath and removing the guilt and stain of sin. With the use of the word *propitiation* here, John is emphasizing that God sent Jesus to remove the guilt we had incurred because of our sins so that we might have eternal life.[11] How glorious is this news!

---

[10] Marshall, *Epistles of John*, 212.

[11] Kruse, *Letters of John*, 161.

Some people say that a God of love can't be a God of
wrath, and therefore propitiation and love cannot go together. But, as James Denney put it, "So far from finding any
kind of contrast between love and propitiation, the apostle
can convey no idea of love to anyone except by pointing to
the propitiation—love is what is manifested there; and he
can give no account of the propitiation but by saying, 'Behold what manner of love'; For him, to say 'God is love' is
exactly the same as to say, 'God has in his Son made atonement for the sin of the world.' If the propitiatory death of
Jesus is eliminated from the love of God, it might be unfair
to say that the love of God is robbed of all meaning, but it is
certainly robbed of its apostolic meaning. It has no longer
that meaning which goes deeper than sin, sorrow, and
death, and which recreates life in the adoring joy, wonder,
and purity of the first epistle of John."[12]

Love is characterized by self-sacrifice and action done on
behalf of others.[13] From this verse, we realize that true love is
best born out of gratitude and that in Christ's love, we are
empowered to love others.

> 11-12 *Beloved, if God so loved us, we also ought to love one anoth-
> er. No one has ever seen God; if we love one another, God abides in us
> and his love is perfected in us.*

John says that if God so loved us [i.e., loved us in this way
(*houtōs*)], we also ought to love one another. This is very similar to what he wrote in his gospel. The New English translation is better than most translations in getting at what John

---

[12] James Denney, *The Death of Christ* (London, 1951), 152 quoted in Marshall, *Epistles of John*, 215.

[13] Marshall, *Epistles of John*, 214.

means in John 3:16: *"For this is the way (houtōs) God loved the world: He gave his one and only Son, so that everyone who believes in him will not perish but have eternal life."*

The false teachers may have claimed to have had some kind of direct vision of God, but John rebuts, *"No one has ever seen God."* God is invisible:

> John 1:18—*No one has ever seen God; the only God, who is at the Father's side, he has made him known.*
>
> John 5:37—*And the Father who sent me has himself borne witness about me. His voice you have never heard, his form you have never seen.*
>
> 1 Tim. 1:17—*To the King of ages, immortal, invisible, the only God, be honor and glory forever and ever. Amen.*
>
> 1 Tim. 6:16—*[God] who alone has immortality, who dwells in unapproachable light, whom no one has ever seen or can see. To him be honor and eternal dominion. Amen.*

As we have seen repeatedly, loving others is an essential part of loving God. John snubs his nose at mystical experience as the high point in religion. For John, true spirituality is very practical. This is how we fully experience the love of God. It consists of believing in the Son and loving one another. We don't find God by withdrawing from the world; we find him in giving ourselves for one another. As Stott writes, "No one who has been to the cross and seen God's immeasurable and unmerited love displayed there can go back to a life of selfishness."[14]

This is the second of four references in 1 John to God's love being perfected in us:

---

[14] Stott, *Letters of John*, 164.

1 John 2:5—*But whoever keeps his word, in him truly the love of God is perfected. By this we may know that we are in him.*

1 John 4:17—*By this is love perfected with us, so that we may have confidence for the day of judgment, because as he is so also are we in this world.*

1 John 4:18—*There is no fear in love, but perfect love casts out fear. For fear has to do with punishment, and whoever fears has not been perfected in love.*

Chapter 9

1 John 4:13-5:5

By this we know that we abide in him and he in us, because he has given us of his Spirit. And we have seen and testify that the Father has sent his Son to be the Savior of the world. Whoever confesses that Jesus is the Son of God, God abides in him, and he in God. So we have come to know and to believe the love that God has for us. God is love, and whoever abides in love abides in God, and God abides in him. By this is love perfected with us, so that we may have confidence for the day of judgment, because as he is so also are we in this world. There is no fear in love, but perfect love casts out fear. For fear has to do with punishment, and whoever fears has not been perfected in love. We love because he first loved us. If anyone says, "I love God," and hates his brother, he is a liar; for he who does not love his brother whom he has seen cannot love God whom he has not seen. And this commandment we have from him: whoever loves God must also love his brother. Everyone who believes that Jesus is the Christ has been born of God, and everyone who loves the Father loves whoever has been born of him. By this we know that we love the children of God, when we love God and obey his commandments. For this is the love of God, that we keep his commandments. And his commandments are not burdensome. For everyone who has been born of God overcomes the world. And this is the victory that has overcome the world—our faith. Who is it that overcomes the world except the one who believes that Jesus is the Son of God?

In this section, the three tests of belief, love, and obedience are interwoven throughout.

13-15 *By this we know that we abide in him and he in us, because he has given us of his Spirit. And we have seen and testify that the*

Father has sent his Son to be the Savior of the world. Whoever con-
fesses that Jesus is the Son of God, God abides in him, and he in God.

God dwells in us through the Spirit. In the previous verse
(v. 12), John has just said that God lives in us if we love one
another. Here we know that he lives in us because of the
Spirit he has given us. So we have both an external test and
an internal test. We have seen this balance throughout the
letter. We know God lives in us if we love our fellow Christians, and we know he lives in us by the Spirit. Of course, it
is the Spirit who enables and motivates love for others. This
is one of the central points of Galatians 5. The firstfruit of the
Spirit listed is *love.*

We have seen from this letter that assurance has multiple
aspects.[1] There is the cross, true belief, love of one another,
and the witness of the Spirit (Rom. 8:16).

The Spirit also teaches the truth about Jesus. It is only by
the Spirit that we acknowledge Jesus as the Son of God and
that we live in love. As Paul said in 1 Corinthians 12:3,
"Therefore I want you to understand that no one speaking in the
Spirit of God ever says 'Jesus is accursed!' and no one can say 'Je-
sus is Lord' except in the Holy Spirit."

After the mention of the Spirit in verse 13, verse 14 mentions the Father's sending of the Son. With eyes to see, the
Trinity is all over the pages of the New Testament. The *world*
in verse 14 refers to sinful society, estranged from God and

---

[1] Marshall, *Epistles of John*, 219. Kruse shows that in this letter, assurance
   is based on God's testimony to his Son, righteous living, loving action
   and concern, asking according to God's will, the love command, and
   the Spirit's testimony to Christ; Kruse, *Letters of John*, 198-200.

under the rule of Satan (1 John 5:19).[2] John uses the phrase *Savior of the world* in his gospel as well: *"They said to the woman, 'It is no longer because of what you said that we believe, for we have heard for ourselves, and we know that this is indeed the Savior of the world'"* (4:42). By *world* in that context, John means Jews and Samaritans.

When verse 15 speaks of acknowledging that Jesus is the Son of God, John certainly means to agree with the apostolic teaching that Jesus is both God and man, but it is also *obedient* trust in him.[3] Acknowledgment of Jesus as the world's true Lord (i.e., Messiah) can never remain *merely* intellectual.

16 *So we have come to know and to believe the love that God has for us. God is love, and whoever abides in love abides in God, and God abides in him.*

God is love. To be godly is to live in love. Of course, it is not the case that we must abide in love *in order to* abide in God. Love for others is the proof or result of abiding in God. As C.H. Dodd put it, "The expression 'to remain in love' is suggestive rather than exact. It is not clear whether the meaning is 'to continue to live as the objects of God's love,' or 'to continue to love God,' or 'to continue to love our brothers.' It is in fact impossible, according to the teaching both of this epistle and of the fourth gospel, to make a clear separation between these three modes or manifestations of love. The energy of love discharges itself along lines which form a triangle, whose points are God, self, and neighbor: but the source of all love is God, of whom alone it can be said that he *is* love. Whether we love God or our neighbor, it

[2] Stott, *Letters of John*, 167.

[3] Marshall, *Epistles of John*, 220-21.

is God's love that is at work in us—assuming, that is, that our love is that authentic *agapē* which is exemplified in God's gift of his Son, and in Christ's sacrifice for us all."[4]

> 17-18 *By this is love perfected with us, so that we may have confidence for the day of judgment, because as he is so also are we in this world. There is no fear in love, but perfect love casts out fear. For fear has to do with punishment, and whoever fears has not been perfected in love.*

In 4:12, John had mentioned love being perfected as well: *"No one has ever seen God; if we love one another, God abides in us and his love is perfected in us."* Above, we mentioned that there are several bases for assurance. Here we see that our confidence on the day of judgment is in part based upon our Christ-likeness. In 2:28, he said that we would have confidence by continuing in him. In our verse here, though, John says we will have confidence if we are like Jesus in this world. Jesus is offered as an example several times in this short letter:

> 1 John 1:7—*But if we walk in the light, as he is in the light, we have fellowship with one another, and the blood of Jesus his Son cleanses us from all sin.*

> 1 John 2:6—*Whoever says he abides in him ought to walk in the same way in which he walked.*

> 1 John 3:3—*And everyone who thus hopes in him purifies himself as he is pure.*

> 1 John 3:7—*Little children, let no one deceive you. Whoever practices righteousness is righteous, as he is righteous.*

---

[4] C.H. Dodd, *The Johannine Epistles,* Moffatt New Testament Commentary (London, 1946), 117, quoted in Marshall, *Epistles of John,* 222.

In these verses, is John thinking of God's love for us or our love for God? Probably both. In a relationship of mutual love, there is no room for fear.[5] *Perfect love* is God's love for us, but that cannot be separated from our love for him.[6] We love *because* he loved us. As Raymond Brown puts it, "There is probably continuity with the theme of love that has run through the unit: an outgoing love that comes from God, is manifested in Jesus, gives us life, and remains in us actively manifesting itself in love of others and of God."[7]

We can't love God and fear him because fear has to do with punishment. The word for *punishment* (*kolasis*) is only used one other time in the New Testament in Matt. 25:46: "*And these will go away into eternal punishment, but the right- eous into eternal life.*"[8] We are loved by God. We are his chil- dren (1 John 3:1) so we need not fear his punishment. We have an advocate, Jesus, who was the propitiation for our sins (1 John 2:1-2). As Kruse puts it, "When the realization of God's love for us in Christ penetrates our minds and spirits, then we are perfected in love so that fear of God's judgment is removed."[9]

19 *We love because he first loved us.*

God is the initiator in this relationship. In 4:10, John said, "*In this is love, not that we have loved God but that he loved us and sent his Son to be the propitiation for our sins.*" Knowing how richly God has sovereignly loved us deepens our love

---

[5] Marshall, *Epistles of John,* 224.

[6] Kruse, *Letters of John,* 168.

[7] Raymond Brown, *Epistles of John* (New York: Doubleday, 1982), 530.

[8] Kruse, *Letters of John,* 168.

[9] Ibid., 169.

for him. All who have been gripped by the sovereignty of grace know this to be true.

20-21 *If anyone says, "I love God," and hates his brother, he is a liar; for he who does not love his brother whom he has seen cannot love God whom he has not seen. And this commandment we have from him: whoever loves God must also love his brother.*

If anyone claims to love God, this love must be worked out in community. Otherwise you are a liar. John is fond of pointing out the untruthfulness of false statements:

1 John 1:10—*If we say we have not sinned, we make him a liar, and his word is not in us.*

1 John 2:4—*Whoever says "I know him" but does not keep his commandments is a liar, and the truth is not in him.*

1 John 2:22—*Who is the liar but he who denies that Jesus is the Christ? This is the antichrist, he who denies the Father and the Son.*

1 John 5:10—*Whoever believes in the Son of God has the testimony in himself. Whoever does not believe God has made him a liar, because he has not believed in the testimony that God has borne concerning his Son.*

One cannot claim to love God and not love their fellow Christians. As we will see in 5:1, everyone who loves the Father loves the children of the Father. As Calvin put it, "It is a false boast when anyone says that he loves God but neglects his image which is before his eyes."[10] John Stott agrees, writing, "Every claim to love God is a delusion if it is not accompanied by unselfish and practical love for our brothers and sisters (3:17-18)."[11] We have seen how important this is

---

[10] Quoted in Stott, *Letters of John*, 171.

[11] Stott, *Letters of John*, 171.

for John. It must become just as important for us. Consider the pervasiveness of this fundamental command once more:

1 John 4:12—*No one has ever seen God; if we love one another, God abides in us and his love is perfected in us.*

John 13:34-35—*A new commandment I give to you, that you love one another: just as I have loved you, you also are to love one another. By this all people will know that you are my disciples, if you have love for one another.*

John 15:12—*This is my commandment, that you love one another as I have loved you.*

John 15:17—*These things I command you, so that you will love one another.*

This is the Great Commandment. Matthew records the following encounter: *"Teacher, which is the great commandment in the Law?" And he said to him, "You shall love the Lord your God with all your heart and with all your soul and with all your mind. This is the great and first commandment. And a second is like it: You shall love your neighbor as yourself. On these two commandments depend all the Law and the Prophets"* (22:36-40). Jesus united Deuteronomy 6:4 and Leviticus 19:18 to show that love for God and love for neighbor necessarily go hand in hand. We cannot separate what Jesus has joined.

What this means in practical terms is that Christians must make the members of their local church a priority. We must be involved in one another's lives. We must check on those whom you haven't seen in a while. Who has not been at home group or women's group lately? Do you pray for your brothers and sisters? Do you seek to serve them? Do you have people over? Do you make church members a priority in your life? Hospitality is the lost art in American Christianity. Often we are embarrassed of our homes, but this is a poor excuse. Proverbs 15:17 says, *"Better is a dinner of herbs where love is than a fattened ox and hatred with it."* Invite people over and have soup to the glory of God.

> 5:1-3—*Everyone who believes that Jesus is the Christ has been born of God, and everyone who loves the Father loves whoever has been born of him. By this we know that we love the children of God, when we love God and obey his commandments. For this is the love of God, that we keep his commandments. And his commandments are not burdensome.*

This verse makes it clear that believing that Jesus is the Christ is a *sign* of being born of God, as is loving one another (1 John 4:7). Everyone who presently believes *has been* born of God. Again we see the beautiful sovereignty of grace. Even our faith is a gift from the Great Giver (Eph. 2:8-10).

John repeats himself. He wants us to realize how vital it is to love God and love one another. He uses a metaphor from natural experience here. If you love and respect a man who is a father, you will also love and respect his child.[12] One of my best friends recently had a baby boy. Unfortunately, we live miles apart so I have only seen pictures on the web. Even though I have yet to meet this little one, I love him because I love his father.

As should be clear by now, love for John is not an emotion but is always practical and active. Love for fellow Christians expresses itself with actions and in truth.[13] Love and obedience go hand in hand. Jesus made this clear in the Upper Room Discourse. John 14:15 says, *"If you love me, you will keep my commandments."* In John 14:21, Jesus said that the one

---

[12] Kruse, *Letters of John,* 171.

[13] Stott, *Letters of John,* 173.

who has and keeps his commandments is the one who loves him. John is a faithful interpreter of the mind of Jesus.

It is not beyond our ability to obey. His commandments are not burdensome. Matthew 11:28-30 reads, *"Come to me, all who labor and are heavy laden, and I will give you rest. Take my yoke upon you, and learn from me, for I am gentle and lowly in heart, and you will find rest for your souls. For my yoke is easy, and my burden is light."* His commandments are not a burden but a joy because when we obey him, we are doing what we were created for.

> 4-5 *For everyone who has been born of God overcomes the world. And this is the victory that has overcome the world—our faith. Who is it that overcomes the world except the one who believes that Jesus is the Son of God?*

Those born of God overcome the world. Those born of God have the empowering presence of God, who enables them to overcome the world.

By *world* John lumps together all the transitory powers that make obedience difficult (see 1 John 2:15-17), whether it be moral pressures, secular attitudes, persecution, or heresy.[14] We who have been born of God have overcome the worldly tendency to satisfy our own sinful desires, and as a result, we are free to show love to others; in this way we will fulfill God's command.[15]

In 1 John 5:1, Jesus is the Christ. Here, Jesus is the Son of God. For the New Testament, the two are synonymous.[16] John Stott provides a nice summary of this section: "Chris-

---

[14] Ibid., 174.

[15] Kruse, *Letters of John,* 173.

[16] Marshall, *Epistles of John,* 231; Kruse, *Letters of John,* 174.

tian believers are God's children, born from above. God's children are loved by all who love God. Those who love God also keep his commands. They keep his commands because they overcome the world, and they overcome the world because they are Christian believers, born from above."[17]

---

[17] Stott, *Letters of John*, 175.

Chapter 10

1 John 5:6-21

This is he who came by water and blood—Jesus Christ; not by the water only but by the water and the blood. And the Spirit is the one who testifies, because the Spirit is the truth. For there are three that testify: the Spirit and the water and the blood; and these three agree. If we receive the testimony of men, the testimony of God is greater, for this is the testimony of God that he has borne concerning his Son. Whoever believes in the Son of God has the testimony in himself. Whoever does not believe God has made him a liar, because he has not believed in the testimony that God has borne concerning his Son. And this is the testimony, that God gave us eternal life, and this life is in his Son. Whoever has the Son has life; whoever does not have the Son of God does not have life. I write these things to you who believe in the name of the Son of God that you may know that you have eternal life. And this is the confidence that we have toward him, that if we ask anything according to his will he hears us. And if we know that he hears us in whatever we ask, we know that we have the requests that we have asked of him. If anyone sees his brother committing a sin not leading to death, he shall ask, and God will give him life—to those who commit sins that do not lead to death. There is sin that leads to death; I do not say that one should pray for that. All wrongdoing is sin, but there is sin that does not lead to death. We know that everyone who has been born of God does not keep on sinning, but he who was born of God protects him, and the evil one does not touch him. We know that we are from God, and the whole world lies in the power of the evil one. And we know that the Son of God has come and has given us understanding, so that we may know him who is true; and we are in him who is true, in his Son Jesus Christ. He is the true God and eternal life. Little children, keep yourselves from idols.

6-8 This is he who came by water and blood—Jesus Christ; not by the water only but by the water and the blood. And the Spirit is the one who testifies, because the Spirit is the truth. For there are three that testify: the Spirit and the water and the blood; and these three agree.

This verse is somewhat unclear so we must keep in mind the nature of the false teaching that John was dealing with. Recall that it was some sort of Gnosticism before there was Gnosticism (proto-Gnosticism). They may have believed that the Christ descended upon Jesus at baptism, but left him before the crucifixion. John says he came by water and blood.

John is emphasizing the humanity of Jesus. Although some have thought John was referring to the sacraments or to the blood and water that came out of Jesus' side (cf. John 19:34-35),[1] he is probably referring to the water of Jesus' baptism and the blood of his crucifixion. In 1 John 1:7, John referred to the blood of Jesus cleansing us from sin. There, the cross is clearly in mind. Jesus came *by* (literally *through* (*di*)] water and blood. These must be references to historical events in the life of Jesus. John is stressing the unity of the earthly career of Jesus.[2] As Marshall puts it, "He is claiming that Jesus Christ truly was baptized and truly died on the cross."[3]

The Holy Spirit testifies, and it is worth noting that testifying is something persons do. The Holy Spirit is a person, not an impersonal force or power. The Spirit moved the

---

[1] Thielman, *Theology of the New Testament*, 539.

[2] Stott, *Letters of John*, 178. The false teachers may have taught that the Christ descended upon the earthly Jesus at his baptism and departed before the cross (hence "not by water only"). John disagrees.

[3] Marshall, *Epistles of John*, 232; Stott, *Letters of John*, 178.

writers of the Old Testament to point to Christ and worked
in and through his life.[4]

He is the Spirit of truth:

> 1 John 4:6—*We are from God. Whoever knows God listens to us;
> whoever is not from God does not listen to us. By this we know the
> Spirit of truth and the spirit of error.*

> John 14:16-17—*And I will ask the Father, and he will give you
> another Helper, to be with you forever, even the Spirit of truth, whom
> the world cannot receive, because it neither sees him nor knows him.
> You know him, for he dwells with you and will be in you.*

> John 15:26—*But when the Helper comes, whom I will send to you
> from the Father, the Spirit of truth, who proceeds from the Father, he
> will bear witness about me.*

> John 16:13—*When the Spirit of truth comes, he will guide you
> into all the truth, for he will not speak on his own authority, but
> whatever he hears he will speak, and he will declare to you the things
> that are to come.*

Those who remember the KJV will be aware of the men-
tion of the Trinity in this verse. It says, *"For there are three that
bear record in heaven, the Father, the Word, and the Holy Ghost:
and these three are one."* This form of the text does not appear
in any reputable modern translations for good reason. The
words are not found in any early Greek manuscripts and are
not quoted by any early church writers. This is a glaring
omission considering all the debates centering on the Trinity
in the first centuries of the church. If this were an original
reading, surely it would have been a key proof text.[5]

---

[4] Ibid., 235.

[5] See Marshall, *Epistles of John*, 236; Stott, *Letters of John*, 180.

Erasmus, the man who put together the first Greek New Testament, did not include these words, but there was uproar in some Roman Catholic circles. Erasmus responded that he did not include it because he had found no Greek manuscripts which had that reading. Conveniently, a Greek manuscript including that reading appeared in 1520, so Erasmus used it in his next edition. More manuscripts were copied but none of them appear to have been earlier than the sixteenth century.[6]

> 9-11 *If we receive the testimony of men, the testimony of God is greater, for this is the testimony of God that he has borne concerning his Son. Whoever believes in the Son of God has the testimony in himself. Whoever does not believe God has made him a liar, because he has not believed in the testimony that God has borne concerning his Son. And this is the testimony, that God gave us eternal life, and this life is in his Son.*

Jesus embodies the revelation of God. He *is* God's testimony. He is the Word of God made flesh. The testimony is passed down to us through the apostles.[7]

To reject Jesus is to call God a liar, and that is no small thing. Unbelief is sin. Jesus is Lord and demands allegiance and will get glory. First Peter 2:12 reads, *"Keep your conduct among the Gentiles honorable, so that when they speak against you as evildoers, they may see your good deeds and glorify God on the day of visitation."* By *day of visitation* I think Peter is referring to the day of judgment. Philippians 2:10 reads, *"So that at the name of Jesus every knee should bow, in heaven and on earth and*

---

[6] Ibid., See Daniel B. Wallace, "Why I Do Not Think the King James Bible Is the Best Translation Available Today." I accessed this article somewhere online several years ago but cannot recall when or where.

[7] Kruse, *Letters of John*, 181.

under the earth, and every tongue confess that Jesus Christ is Lord, to the glory of God the Father." This is an astounding statement. Every single knee will bow and every single tongue will acknowledge the supremacy of King Jesus — now willingly or then in destruction.

12 *Whoever has the Son has life; whoever does not have the Son of God does not have life.*

Jesus is eternal life. In 1 John 1:2, Jesus is called *the life* that was made manifest and that the apostles had seen and touched. In 1 John 5:20, John says that Jesus *"is the true God and eternal life."* To have Jesus is to have the life of the age to come (*zōēn aiōnion*). We have seen above that in this letter, eternal life is almost always referring to a present experience for believers.[8] This needs to be taught, re-taught, and taught again in our pluralistic culture. Jesus is the only way to salvation (John 11:25, 14:6, Acts 4:12, 1 Tim. 2:5). The alternative is clear and uncompromising.

13 *I write these things to you who believe in the name of the Son of God that you may know that you have eternal life.*

John has given us many of his purposes in writing this letter, but this seems to be the main one. At the conclusion of his gospel, he wrote, *"But these are written so that you may believe that Jesus is the Christ, the Son of God, and that by believing you may have life in his name"* (John 20:31). His gospel was written more for evangelistic purposes, but his letter is written to strengthen Christian believers.

14-15 *And this is the confidence that we have toward him, that if we ask anything according to his will he hears us. And if we know*

---

[8] Ibid., 184.

that he hears us in whatever we ask, we know that we have the re-
quests that we have asked of him.

We have confidence that God hears our prayers when they are in accord with his will. In Mark 11:24, Jesus says, *"Therefore I tell you, whatever you ask in prayer, believe that you have received it, and it will be yours."* John Stott writes, "Prayer is not a convenient device for imposing our will upon God, or for bending his will to ours, but the prescribed way of subordinating our will to his. It is by prayer that we seek God's will, embrace it and align ourselves with it. Every true prayer is a variation on the theme 'your will be done.'"[9]

How do we know if we are praying in accord with God's will? By the Word. Pray Scripture. As you read, turn the sentences into prayers. This is a great way to learn to pray biblically based prayers.

Of course, we often only know God's will in a general way. Often we do not know the specifics of God's will for our lives or for the lives of the people we are interceding for.

16-17 *If anyone sees his brother committing a sin not leading to death, he shall ask, and God will give him life—to those who commit sins that do not lead to death. There is sin that leads to death; I do not say that one should pray for that. All wrongdoing is sin, but there is sin that does not lead to death.*

Okay, so what is this sin that leads to death? While we may be uncertain as to what this verse means, John's readers would have known exactly what he was referring to since he felt no need to explain it. By sin that leads to death, does he mean a specific sin?[10] Is it one of the seven deadly sins?

---

[9] Stott, *Letters of John*, 185.

[10] See Stott's helpful analysis, *Letters of John*, 187-88.

There is no New Testament evidence for this view. Does John mean apostasy? Probably not, since John has already said that those born of God cannot continue in sin (3:6-9), let alone fall away completely. Or does he mean blasphemy against the Holy Spirit as mentioned in the Gospels, which is the deliberate rejection of obvious truth? It is the attributing of the work of God to Satan (Matt. 12, Mark 3).

By death, he probably does not mean that the sinner physically dies when they commit this sin because every sinner faces physical death because of sin (Rom. 6:23); John probably means spiritual death (that is, sin that is utterly incompatible with being born of God). In this letter, we have seen this to include denying that Jesus is the Son of God, refusing to obey God's commandments, loving the world, and hatred of fellow believers. Sin that leads to death is deliberately refusing to believe that Jesus is the Christ, refusing to follow God's commands, and refusing to love one's brothers and sisters.[11] He is referring to the false teachers who had gone out to show they were not "of us." He is talking about those who deny the Son and do not possess the Father, those whose Father is the devil, those who are the spirit of antichrist. Sin that does not lead to death would include the sins that are committed unwittingly. We still believe in Jesus as Lord, still strive to obey, and still seek to love.

John's advice not to pray for them has Old Testament precedent. Jeremiah is told not to pray for Israel because their sins were so repugnant.

---

[11] Marshall, *Epistles of John*, 247-48.

Jer. 7:16—*As for you, do not pray for this people, or lift up a cry or prayer for them, and do not intercede with me, for I will not hear you.*

Jer. 11:14—*Therefore do not pray for this people, or lift up a cry or prayer on their behalf, for I will not listen when they call to me in the time of their trouble.*

Jer. 14:11—*The LORD said to me: "Do not pray for the welfare of this people."*

Jesus also refuses to pray for the world in John 17:9.[12]

We should pray for our brothers and sisters frequently, and especially, writes John, when you *see* them in sin. The verse literally says, "He will ask and will give him life." John is not commanding them to pray for their brothers and sisters. He is saying it will be a natural and spontaneous reaction for those who are in Christ.[13]

18 *We know that everyone who has been born of God does not keep on sinning, but he who was born of God protects him, and the evil one does not touch him.*

This is similar to what we saw above in chapter 3. "*No one who abides in him keeps on sinning*" (3:6). "*No one born of God makes a practice of sinning*" (3:9). As with 1 John 3, so here we see from the context that John does not mean sinlessness. He has just finished exhorting us to pray for fellow believers who sin. John is referring to our habitual practice, the trajectory of our lives.

Jude 1:24-25: *Now to him who is able to keep you from stumbling and to present you blameless before the presence of his glory with great joy, to the only God, our Savior, through Jesus Christ our Lord,*

---

[12] Kruse, *Letters of John*, 193.

[13] Stott, *Letters of John*, 185-86.

be glory, majesty, dominion, and authority, before all time and now and forever. Amen.

We must be kept. We cannot compete with the evil one, but the One born of God came to destroy the devil's work (1 John 3:8) and he who is in us is greater than he who is in the world (1 John 4:4). John 10:28 says, *"I give them eternal life, and they will never perish, and no one will snatch them out of my hand."*

19-20 *We know that we are from God, and the whole world lies in the power of the evil one. And we know that the Son of God has come and has given us understanding, so that we may know him who is true; and we are in him who is true, in his Son Jesus Christ. He is the true God and eternal life.*

Satan is not to be joked about. The evil one cannot touch the Christian, but the world is helplessly in his grasp. Ephesians 2:2 calls him the *"prince of the power of the air."* Second Corinthians 4:4 calls him the *"god of this world."* John 14:30 and 16:11 speak of him as the *"ruler of this world."* Luke 4:5-6 reads, *"And the devil took him up and showed him all the kingdoms of the world in a moment of time, and said to him, 'To you I will give all this authority and their glory, for it has been delivered to me, and I give it to whom I will.'"* Notice that Jesus did not dispute the offer. Unbelievers are in bondage to hostile powers of darkness. They are captive in Satan's domain. There is no third category.[14]

As we have seen, *world* in John refers to human society in terms of its organized opposition to God. As Clinton Arnold writes, "It appears that while Satan's influence and control is

[14] Ibid., 193.

primarily over people, it also extends to human institutions and organizations, the social and political order."[15]

The Son has come and given us understanding. God has revealed himself to us in his Son. Christianity is a religion that is based on revelation from God. It is a gracious gift to have revelation! Left to ourselves, we are all doomed, damned, hopeless, and helpless.

Jesus is the true God and eternal life (cf. John 1:1).

21 *Little children, keep yourselves from idols.*

This abrupt ending has puzzled commentators. The mention of idols comes out of nowhere. Nowhere in the letter has John mentioned the worship of physical images or false gods. However, John is warning his readers of false conceptions of god. They, and we, must keep ourselves from following, trusting, obeying, or revering anyone or anything other than the one true God and his Son Jesus Christ. As Ben Merkle has written, "The ending of John's letter reiterates and emphasizes the main point of his letter and should not be read as introducing a new thought. That is, John is stating that those who fail the three tests mentioned throughout the letter (the tests of belief, righteousness, and love) are, in essence, guilty of idolatry. To embrace a form of Christianity that allows one to deny the truth about Jesus, not live a godly life, or not love others, is to create an idol—and that is

---

[15] Clinton Arnold, *Powers of Darkness* (Downers Grove, IL: IVP, 1992), 81. This book is a superb study of the principalities and powers in Paul's letters.

something all Christian must constantly guard themselves against."[16]

John deliberately concludes with a warning to stay away from idols. The verse before this one said that Jesus is the true God. To worship any other Jesus than the one the apostles saw, touched, and heard is to worship a false Jesus. It is to worship an idol. Dear children, keep yourselves from idols.

---

[16] Benjamin J. Merkle, "First John 5:21 as an Interpretive Key to the Epistle." A Paper Presented to the Evangelical Theological Society (November 18, 2010, Atlanta, GA), 15. I am grateful for Dr. Merkle emailing me a copy of his paper.

Bibliography

Arnold, Clinton. *Three Crucial Questions About Spiritual Warfare.* Grand Rapids: Baker Books, 1997.

_____. *The Powers of Darkness.* Downers Grove, IL: IVP, 1992.

Boyd, Gregory. "Christus Victor View." In *The Nature of the Atonement,* edited by James Beilby and Paul R. Eddy. Downers Grove, IL: IVP Academic, 2006.

Brown, Raymond. *The Epistles of John.* New York: Doubleday, 1982.

Carson, D.A. and Douglas Moo. *An Introduction to the New Testament.* Grand Rapids: Zondervan, 2005.

Carson, D.A. "Atonement in Romans 3:21-26." In *The Glory of the Atonement,* edited by Charles E. Hill and Frank A. James III. Downers Grove, IL: IVP, 2009.

_____. *The Gospel According to John.* Grand Rapids: Eerdmans, 1991.

_____. "The Johannine Letters" in *New Dictionary of Biblical Theology,* edited by T. Desmond Alexander, Brian Rosner, D.A. Carson, and Graeme Goldsworthy. Downers Grove, IL: IVP, 2000.

Chalke, Steve. *The Lost Message of Jesus.* Grand Rapids: Zondervan, 2003.

Cole, Graham A. "Exodus 34, the Middoth, and the Doctrine of God." *SBJT 12.3.* Fall 2003.

_____. *God the Peacemaker.* Downers Grove, IL: IVP, 2009.

Denney, James. *The Death of Christ.* London, 1951.

Dockery, D.S. "Fruit of the Spirit." In *Dictionary of Paul and His Letters.* Downers Grove, IL: IVP, 1993.

Dodd, C.H. *The Johannine Epistles.* Moffatt New Testament Commentary. London, 1946.

Fee, Gordon. *Paul, the Spirit, and the People of God.* Peabody, MA: Hendrickson, 1996.

Ferguson, Sinclair. *The Holy Spirit.* Downers Grove, IL: IVP, 1996.

Gorman, Michael. *Cruciformity.* Grand Rapids: Eerdmans, 2001.

Hays, Richard B. *The Moral Vision of the New Testament.* New York: HarperOne, 1996.

Kruse, Colin. *The Letters of John.* Grand Rapids: Eerdmans, 2000.

Letham, Robert. *The Work of Christ.* Downers Grove, IL: IVP, 1993.

Linne, Shai. *The Atonement.* Lamp Mode Recordings, 2008.

Luther, Martin. "Ninety-Five Theses." In *Martin Luther's Basic Theological Writings,* edited by Timothy F. Lull. Minneapolis: Fortress, 1989.

Marshall, I. Howard. *The Epistles of John.* Grand Rapids: Eerdmans, 1978.

McKnight, Scot. *A Community Called Atonement.* Nashville: Abingdon, 2007.

Merkle, Benjamin. "First John 5:21 as an Interpretive Key to the Epistle." A Paper Presented to the Evangelical Theological Society (November 18, 2010, Atlanta, GA).

Morris, Leon. *The Apostolic Preaching of the Cross.* Grand Rapids: Eerdmans, 1965.

Mouw, Richard. *When the Kings Come Marching In.* Grand Rapids: Eerdmans, 2002.

Owen, John. *The Death of Death in the Death of Christ.* Edinburgh: Banner of Truth, 2002.

Piper, John. *Finally Alive.* Scotland: Christian Focus, 2009.

Rosner, Brian. *Beyond Greed.* Australia: Matthias Media, 2004.

Schrage, Wolfgang. *The Ethics of the New Testament,* translated by David E. Green. Philadelphia: Fortress Press, 1982.

Schreiner, Thomas R. *New Testament Theology.* Grand Rapids: Baker, 2008.

Stott, John. *The Letters of John.* Downers Grove, IL: IVP Academic, 1988.

Thielman, Frank. *Theology of the New Testament.* Grand Rapids: Zondervan, 2005.

Tripp, Paul David. *What Did You Expect?* Wheaton, IL: Crossway, 2010.

Wells, David. *Losing Our Virtue.* Grand Rapids: Eerdmans, 1998.

White, A. Blake. *The Law of Christ.* Frederick, MD: New Covenant Media, 2010.

White, R.E.O. *Biblical Ethics.* Atlanta: John Knox Press, 1979.

Wright, N.T. *After You Believe.* New York: HarperOne, 2010.

_____. *Evil and the Justice of God.* Downers Grove, IL: IVP, 2006.

www.ingramcontent.com/pod-product-compliance
Lightning Source LLC
LaVergne TN
LVHW051642080426
835511LV00016B/2439